GOD, GRIT
& HUMOR

GOD, GRIT & HUMOR

ALVIN DOTEN

HARLO PRESS   DETROIT, MICH.

Printed by Harlo Press, 50 Victor Avenue, Detroit, Michigan 48203

This book is dedicated
to
the many folks
who helped me at life's task.

The author is grateful to the following for their help and permissions: Bentley Historical Library, University of Michigan; Coordinator of Archives, Ferris State College; Upper Peninsula Travel and Recreational Association; Detroit Conference Historical Society; Sault Ste. Marie Chamber of Commerce; The Rodeheaver Co.; Evangelical Publishers, Toronto; Oklahoma Chamber of Commerce; *Reader's Digest;* Abingdon; *Sunday School Times* Company; Calumet-Laurium Chamber of Commerce; Mildred Pound; Gary LaGuire; Madelyn Strausser; Elaine Renollet; Marne Dyer and Cornelius Beukema of Interlochen.

Any omissions will gladly be corrected in future editions.

CONTENTS

LIST OF ILLUSTRATIONS

GOD, GRIT
& HUMOR

SHOE BOX

I was born at a very young age and weighed-in at two-and-one-half pounds. Later, I remember mother telling me that much of the time they kept me wrapped in cotton, in a shoe box on the opened oven door. I have always been *so* grateful that no one ever shut that oven door!

My legs did not carry me; therefore, I did not walk until I was nearly four! I well remember how very fast I could creep. Following the light stripes in the rag carpet became a game through which I developed my speed. By the time I was four years old I weighed twenty pounds! Little did I dream that one day those little legs that would not carry my weight until I was four years old would snowshoe over portions of the Upper Peninsula of Michigan.

Four families actually went back into the woods west of Standish and cut out homes. The four men worked together as a team, a day at a time. There was no exchange of money, just labor. One of these four men had the smallest sawmill you ever saw. Another had a cow which provided milk for the four families. My father had "Old Lou," a great, big white ox. Anything that was too heavy for the four men to lift became a task that was automatically delegated to "Old Lou!" I remember that dad's white ox was a big fellow, with horns about 15 inches long and a one-inch brass knob on the end of each horn.

My first rides as a boy were on a dray drawn by the big ox. Mother would ride on the dray, with her boy, and dad would walk and talk to the ox. ("Old Lou" was never known to be in a hurry.)

The big pine had been lumbered off the land, which my father had bought at two dollars and fifty cents an acre. Two railroads crossed father's land and joined, just before they left the property. Although the pine was gone, a great deal of hardwood was left; as well as hemlock and cedar. The cedar was valuable for its use as railroad ties and roofing shingles. After the railroads took up their steel, the little mill sawed about sixteen-foot rails out of maple timber and the men spiked those onto the ties.

When the lumbermen who felled the great pines left, they abandoned what was then called "bunk cars." These cars were just frames of heavy timbers on four railroad wheels. The pioneer families took the logs and ties, as well as the smaller trees, for wood. Some of the timber was good enough to be shipped to Bay City, Michigan. The rest of the timber that had been left on these old railroad grades was moved over the wooden rails with father's old white ox. Every now and then they had to install a new wooden rail to keep the track in order. My father ingeniously devised some sort of a contraption for a brake on one of the wheels of the bunk cars. This was to keep the car from running up onto the heels of the ox.

The man in this group who owned the little sawmill built a home of newly unplaned sawed boards. Another of the men built a log home. My father dug up some of the better ties from the old railroad switches. He stood them on end and fastened them together by spiking small saplings at the top and the bottom. Next, they chinked the big cracks with marsh grass and clay. Four-inch boards were put over the joints to keep the rain from washing out the clay. This was home! ("Old Lou" was not forgotten. A small barn for the ox and even a water closet were constructed out of railroad ties!)

I can remember the day on which my father brought home an oil lamp. What a change it was! Up until this time we had always had just three or four lanterns which burned kerosene. One of our daily chores had been to clean the chimney and trim the wicks. If we did not do this regularly the lanterns were not much more than lightning bugs. Anyway, having the new little oil lamp helped us when we went inside after working out-of-doors all day.

One of our first projects was to clear about an acre of ground so the family could raise potatoes, corn and some "garden," as we called it then. Wild berries were plentiful, especially raspberries and blackberries. The wild grass seemed filled with strawberries. About two miles away was a small two-acre patch of blueberries where one could hardly walk without stepping on the fruit. And did the ground bear crops! I have never seen peas grow as they did on that land. It must have been the potash in the soil from the burning of the refuse of the timber. (As I look back upon it, as far as food went, and in many other respects, also, we lived pretty well.)

A railroad was nearby—about a quarter of a mile from the house. The train would stop at a crossing to put off groceries, blowing the whistle from one-to-four times—according to the family that was to pick them up. One day when I was about six years old I remember that the train whistled four times. That was the call for the Dotens to pick up their groceries. I remember father taking the ox and dray and going to the crossing.

There he picked up flour, a barrel of crackers and a wooden firkin of sugar. This firkin was made of wooden staves and had hoops about it. It had a wooden handle about an inch-and-a-half wide and a quarter-inch thick for a bale. This firkin *has to be* eighty some years old. To this day, it is still in the family. It is painted coral, and holds a six-foot plant. Before the mother of our children died, she promised our youngest daughter this firkin. The daughter lives in San Diego, California. Some day this old treasure will rest in the Hawaii of the mainland. This daughter, Doreen Johnson, lives next door to the Sherwood Wirts. I believe Dr. Wirts served as a journalist for Billy Graham on six continents. He was also editor of *Decision Magazine*.

The four settlers took rough lumber from the small mill and built a schoolhouse, about 12 x 14 feet. There were 11 pupils from the other three families. I was not old enough to begin school. Carrie Velie, the teacher, boarded at our house. That was the contribution that my folks made to the school system. The other three families each paid the teacher five dollars a month.

19

I remember one day when my mother had bought for me, my very first pair of suspenders. When mother took me to school, I rushed up to the teacher and said, "Carrie, see my new suspenders!"

"May I have them?" Carrie asked.

My answer was, "No, Carrie, they are not size enough for you."

TENSIONS

When tensions became too much and too many hard words had been said, Mother would say, "I think now the time has come when we best all go in the front room." (The *all* meant Dad and her boy.) She would read a Psalm. Then mother would pray as we knelt by three chairs. Somehow things straightened themselves out, whatever it was. No one said another word about it. Whatever it was, no one ever brought it up again. We just went on living life like it ought to be lived, and mother went around the house singing and humming to herself. *(AD)*

BOYHOOD HOME, MADE OF OLD RAILROAD TIES
CHINKED WITH MARSH GRASS AND CLAY.

PACK PEDDLER

When I was about five, the three neighbor men were working with father in the woods when a tree they were felling kicked back and broke father's leg. There was no possible way to release him until the other men made two crosscuts in the log with a saw and removed a short section of the big tree. Then, the three men carried him home. As they entered the little house, he said to mother, "Wife, these are not pack peddlers, but they do now have a pack on their backs." (Meaning himself.) One of the men walked eight-and-a-half miles for a doctor. The doctor walked back with him, the same eight-and-a-half miles, making seventeen miles of footwork in all.

While my father was waiting for the doctor to come he asked mother for a hymn book. (My father could sing! I can't, but I expect to sing in the next world.) Previous to this accident my father had been a very rough man. Well, he sang all the hymns that he knew, and those he did not know he read. He finished the book by the time the doctor arrived. (This was my father's transformation. From that day on he worked just as hard or harder at the Christian way than any other task he ever undertook. This was the beginning of a new highway on life's road.)

The doctor came from Sterling, Michigan. I remember he had the other men build a pine box about eight inches in width and three feet long with the foot slanting outward. In this homemade cast he placed the broken leg. I remember well that I was afraid of the doctor. I can see him yet standing in the doorway with a pail in his hand asking for hot water. The doctor was tired. I knew young as I was that something was wrong with him. What I did not know was that he had used brandy to keep him going on the long trip. Father's foot was set crooked so that one foot turned outward, so you always knew when you found those tracks in the woods that Bill Doten had been there.

Two nearby lumber camps took up a collection from their woodsmen and brought my mother $260.00 which was two-thirds of a year's salary at that time.

"God moves in a mysterious way,
His wonders to perform,
He plants His footsteps in the sea
and rides upon the storm."

After many weeks of suffering, the first work my father did was to make a new road through the woods for the county. He would go to work on crutches. Mother would carry his saw, shovel and axe. On his knees he would cut down the trees, make a corduroy and shovel a little earth on the logs. Then mother would carry the tools back home again, while he hobbled home on his crutches.

My father's "dogged" determination was something everybody admired.

You may not have saved a lot of money in your life, but if you have saved a lot of heartaches for other folks, you are a pretty rich man. *(Seth Parker)*

TROUBLES A PLENTY

When I was a little shaver, I insisted on calling dressing (the kind you eat with a chicken or turkey), "wadding." One day when we were being entertained away from home, my father took me out to the woodshed and gave me a good spanking. He had tried for a long time to break me of the habit of calling dressing "wadding." I just never took him serious enough and when I embarrassed him again by using the term "wadding" when we were dining in a most respectable home, he reminded me in a nonverbal way, by taking me out to the woodshed the second time. Since that day I have been able to remember that wadding belonged to guns and dressing to chicken.

One evening when I was about 10 years old my neighbor chum, Bobby, and I went hunting the cows to bring them home for milking. On the way we passed a log house which the farmer and his family had vacated. The story in the neighborhood was that this particular farmer became discouraged with the land and moved out. Bobby and I gathered stones and played Indian, charged the house and broke all the windows, just to hear the noise of breaking glass and feel the thrill of vandalism of unoccupied property.

The following Sunday the Humphreys came home with us after church for the evening meal. My father had a very choice five-acres of corn and as the custom was in those days with people who visited back and forth, neighbors and friends went out to see each other's gardens and crops. After the folks had looked over the good garden, father took us all through the cornfield. We came out on the western end of the corn acreage, where stood the house with the broken windows. By this time Bobby and I were lagging pretty well back. Soon I heard my father calling,

"Sonny! Do you know anything about these broken windows?" I said, "Yes. Bobby and I played Indian and we broke them." My father was so upset that he took his jackknife and cut blackberry canes and switched me right then and there.

For four days I lay on my stomach. The welts and the cut marks the blackberry canes had made were too tender to touch. I had to stay in bed and could not lie on my back. Mother doctored me. I remember that she used a home made salve made of beeswax and camphor which had a very healing efect.

I did get some consolation out of this experience. Every time my father came into the bedroom he actually cried. This was the only licking I ever received that I felt was overdone. The thing that hurt me most was that Bobby cried and his father carried him. I told the truth and got the briers. Bobby cried and got a "Piggyback ride."

I remember a teacher once asking, "What is the most perishable thing on a train?" Each youngster in the class had a different answer. I was sure I was safe in my thinking. When at last it came my turn I said, "Fruit." "No!" said the teacher. "Newspapers. No one wants yesterday's newspaper."

When I was pretty young, a man who worked for my father asked to take me home to a lumber camp over the weekend. We had to walk three-and-a-half miles to catch the train, then ride four miles on the train, after which we walked four-and-a-half miles to the camp. This added up to four miles of railroading and eight miles of walking. I can still feel my poor little legs on that last four-and-a-half miles.

That night this chap and I slept in a small bedroom off the lumber camp office, a room that was completely covered (ceiling and all) with newspapers. To me this was simply amazing, but I suppose it was the forerunner of good fiberglass insulation! Imagine putting a youngster to sleep in a room like that? There could be no sleep until the lantern was blown out because not all the papers had been put on the wall upside down.

TOBACCO

Could it be that *Kinnikinnik* is the longest word, spelled the same forward and backward, in our language? Anyhow *Kinnikinnik* is the Indian word for tobacco. The white man found tobacco here with the Indians. Columbus must have been the first white man to see Indians smoking tobacco.

Its leaves are sometimes three feet in length and a foot in width. It is grown heavily in the United States and in many other countries, but it cannot stand frost. Taken in large quantities it produces giddiness, faintness, and nausea. It seems to have a sort of poisoning effect, especially noticeable when one begins its use.

My father did not use tobacco, but I can still see my mother who always raised so many, many plants, taking an ash shovel, filling it with hot coals and then sprinkling *Niger Head Tobacco* on the coals and go around holding this under her house plants to kill the lice on her plants.

When I was 12 years of age, Dick, Lou, Bill and I went on an exploring expedition. We wound up, among other things, at an abandoned house where they gave me my first chew of tobacco.

In about 20 minutes they all thought I was going to die, and I wished I could! Finally they took haywire and an old rusty, leaky pail and pulled water out of an abandoned well. They poured pail after pail of this water right over my head trying to make me revive.

I finally did accommodate them.

This experience haunts me in spite of the years in between. I never recall it without thinking of Joe Bigger, a big strong woodsman, who years before worked for my father. Joe chewed tobacco constantly.

At this time we were living in a house built of railroad ties. The floor was made of wide basswood boards which

26

mother scrubbed dutifully twice a week. Joe Bigger was a tremendous worker, a sort of "Paul Bunyan" in the woods. He could lift anything. To my father, Joe was a very valuable man. His "hang-up" was that he was always spitting tobacco juice on mother's clean floor. Finally my father said, "Joe, I have warned you enough times. The next time you spit tobacco juice on my wife's floor you will be fired."

About three days later he spit tobacco juice . . . about halfway up the wall on the railroad ties. Kid-like, I said, "Ma! Joe spit tobacco juice all over your clean wall." That night after supper father counted out Joe's money and told him he was done. Joe packed his few belongings in a bag that the lumberjack called his "turkey" and Joe left with tears in his eyes.

This reminds me of the old conundrum, "Who is the bigger: Mr. Bigger or Mr. Bigger's baby?" Of course most everyone will say, "Mr. Bigger." The fact is the baby is just a *LITTLE* BIGGER!

Die when I may, I want it said by those who knew me best, that I always plucked a thistle and planted a flower where I thought a flower would grow. *(Abraham Lincoln)*

FROZEN INK

When I was a boy about a dozen years old attending a country school, the teacher sometimes forgot to have the wash dish and the water pail emptied at night, in the wintertime. In the morning, we were very apt to find both frozen. This was especially true if we had some 20 to 30° *below* zero weather. After one desperately cold night, we found everything frozen in the morning with the dipper embedded in the ice in the water pail. All our ink bottles were in the same frozen condition.

Someone put the frozen water pail on top of the round-bellied stove to thaw. Alvin caught the idea of putting his bottle of frozen ink by the pail on top of the stove as well, but he forgot to remove the cork. First it thawed alright, then it built up pressure like a steam boiler. After a few minutes there was a terrific pop, much like a willow paper-wad gun, only louder, and with the explosion all the ink in that bottle made a three-foot star-like splatter on the ceiling of the schoolhouse, radiating out from the center, like the *Aurora Borealis!*

The teacher and forty-three others turned their eyes heavenward to see all that spatter from one little bottle. A low whistle went through the room and all eyes were turned toward one white-headed boy (whose father just happened to be the treasurer of the school board).

Father built the scaffold and helped me with a number of coats over the ink until finally he used glue in the paint to keep the ink from coming through and, from there on, the white-headed boy gave that schoolhouse ceiling two coats of white paint.

You can readily guess how this spoiled five Saturdays!

FROZEN INK

THE CIRCUS

When I was about 13, my friend, Dick Bartlett, and I walked two-and-one-half miles one evening. Our journey took us to the home of our friends, Craven and Roy Goodman, a little older than we were. We caught fireflies in the evening, put them in a bottle, and let them loose upstairs in our bedrooms when we were ready to retire. All the bedroom doors in the story were open so we had our own fireworks. We talked and talked instead of sleeping. We were excited about the six-and-one-half miles we had yet to walk the next morning on our way to the circus. We never did get to sleep. We just wanted to be certain we reached the circus grounds on time to see the 10 o'clock free parade of the animals. So we got up at two o'clock in the morning and started walking. We arrived in Standish just as it was coming daylight. We crawled under a circus wagon and went to sleep. We awoke at exactly 12 o'clock noon and, of course, the parade was all over. However, we did get to see the circus in the afternoon.

That night we slept on the floor of the stone depot. The railroad agent who managed the depot must have remembered when he was a boy himself. He did not throw us out, he just ignored us. He asked a few questions and learned we had walked miles, so he let us sleep. When I arrived home the next day my folks were eating their noonday meal and I remember I had 50 cents left. My father said to my mother, "You need not worry about your boy. He'll make it."

After all these years I still love a circus.

DYNAMITE

When I was a boy about 12, the field just north of our house was full of huge pine stumps. Stump-pulling machines were a rarity in those days and most of the removal of these huge stumps, blackened by fire, had to be done by blasting.

The aftereffects of the explosives, that is the smoke and fumes, always made my father desperately ill; so he trained me to handle dynamite: Drill a hole in which to insert from three-to-five sticks; anchor a cap, to which you attached three or four feet of fuse; light this fuse, then run for your life and wait for the explosion.

One day my father was getting sick from the explosives and we had some rather hard words. As a boy I was quite concerned, until I overheard him telling a neighbor that evening, "I had some hard words with a man today and I am really upset. He was one of the best men in this world." I was not supposed to hear it, but I did and I sensed the fact that my father loved me more than I knew!

This brings to mind another neighbor, who lived about a mile-and-a-half away, who had not seen too much schooling and ofttimes got his words confused. But he had a heart of gold. I remember his telling how when he had a big stump to get rid of, he would say, "I'll put seven sticks of damn-a-mite under it, then watch it go."

NAILS, RAISINS & RAINY DAYS

When I was a boy, I slept in an unfinished room upstairs. Why? Well, the schoolteacher who roomed and boarded with us much of the time always had the good room or the guest room, as we would call it today.

It was nothing to awaken on a winter morning and find nearly two inches of snow that had blown through a few cracks and filtered down on the bed.

I was one of those people who, when young, often walked in my sleep. One morning I awakened abruptly because my father called out my name very loudly and this startled me from a walking sleep. I fell, suddenly, over a newly opened keg of nails. They went cascading down the hardwood stairway. It sounded as loud as Niagara Falls— only it was nails, not water.

Guess who inherited a job right after breakfast? Playing 52 pick-up with playing cards was nothing compared to my endless task. They were eight-penny nails. There are just hundreds of them in a keg. (It seemed like millions of them—at the time.)

When I was a boy about 12, I had a chum named Dick. Dick was always challenging me with, "Alvin, I'll wrestle you on my knees." Dick was older and bigger than I and he nearly always won. We were pals who trusted each other, regardless of the difference in our sizes and ages.

Dick and I tried to steal an egg a day and hide them under the railroad bridge until we had enough to buy a treat of some sort after we sold the stolen eggs. Very often we bought seeded raisins.

One Sunday both of our parents went away leaving us to feed the stock and look after the chores. When lunchtime arrived we took a whole pound of raisins, cut it in two in the middle, divided it into two bowls and took them down into the cellar. Here we skimmed cream off the milk pans and with the sugar and cream we ate raisins to our "heart's content." (We did not know that one pound of raisins is equal to four pounds of meat.)

About 3:00 a.m. the next morning we were too sick to care what happened to us. One of our fathers drove about eight-and-a-half miles in a buggy to get a doctor. He arrived about nine o'clock in the morning. By then, we knew we were going to die and wished we would. It was many years before either of us could eat raisins again . . .

Now I like a few in my oatmeal but I don't want to be around watching when they throw the raisins into the porridge.

When I was a boy, the neighbors always slept in on rainy days. After church, in a schoolhouse, on a Sunday afternoon was the only time to sleep in at our house. It had to be a long wet spell to give anyone a chance to sleep in on a weekday.

Father always spent from a day-and-a-half to two days sharpening up every conceivable tool, from paring knives to chisels, draw shaves, axes, shovels, hatchets and whatnots, to the cutting bar on the mowing machine. If the rain made it too dark we had a kerosene lantern for sunshine. Power for the grindstone was furnished by an only son turning a crank on the big grinding wheel. You were almost too tired to eat, but it was the rainy-day schedule on our calendar out in the buggy shed.

The crops needed the rain, but as a boy I was never too fond of it . . . It meant the buggy shed and the grindstone.

Fund-raising sign in front of synagogue: "You can't take it with you, but you could send it on ahead."
(Central Church Bulletin)

BARN RAISING

When I was 12, my father spent a great deal of time preparing timbers for the framing of a hip roof barn. On the day of the barn raising about 20 neighbors came to help. Like the Amish people, they donated their time helping one another. Two good home-cooked meals was their reward for their toil.

The frame timbers were fastened together with wooden pins, one inch in diameter. The timbers which ran lengthwise where the rafters met to form the hip in the roof were called pearline plates. I was small and always had good balancing power so that I could run the pearline plates and deliver the wooden pins to the framers. After the frame was in place and the rafters in position the men began sheeting or boarding up the sides. Often the men were careless and would get to what we call "running the boards" so that when they met in the middle of the wall the last board might be one-half inch wider at the top or bottom (so this last board had to be fitted in what we call a "wedge" shape.)

The morning after the barn raising my father fitted the last wedge shaped board and sent me up with a hatchet to place the blade in the crack between the boards and pry it gently into place. I reefed too hard on the hatchet and broke the handle.

The night had brought a terrific rain and there was at least a foot of water standing in the clay basement; there was a heavy wind blowing from the southwest. I remember my father saying, "Well, you might as well come down, we have to fix a new hatchet handle." About that time the whole barn frame began to squeak and moan and dad said, "Jump, kid, JUMP!" I jumped westward to the ground and the whole structure just dove Northeastward in one terrible crash! If you ever saw a mess of twisted timbers this was it. It was the greatest pile of jackstraws I ever saw. It took father and I over two months to clean up the wreck. Actually, breaking the hatchet handle had saved my life!

There were no telephones, no morning newspapers and it was perhaps a week before we learned that the big rain and the Southwest gale seemed to have been the tail to the devastating Galveston flood. This was the aftermath to one of history's greatest floods.

EMPTY CHAIRS

By the time I was eleven years old, I knew pretty well what I wanted to do on life's highway. So it was that I started to preach to two rows of empty chairs in my mother's kitchen.

Next Saturday, mother was sharp enough to bring out the dining room chairs and fill these chairs with the neighbors' kids, until we had fourteen youths. I had a little artistic trend, so mother tore up an old sheet into 16-inch squares, and I drew pictures on them. I remember one had three crosses on it, one the Rock of Ages, another a red devil with his pitchfork. There were 30-some of these charts. Mother sewed rings on the top corners of these little charts, and we strung them on a wire.

Each Saturday we slid out another chart, and these charts were the basis for my kid sermons. We would sing about three songs, say the Lord's Prayer, and then I would talk about five to eight minutes after which we would sing another three songs. A wise mother always had popcorn or cookies so the neighbors' kids would come back next Saturday. Believe it or not, this went on for two-and-a-half years. *(AD)*

HOMEMADE CASKETS

In the early days when the four families together cut homes out of the woods they would take the brush from the fallen trees and by piling the brush about five feet high, a fence would be formed in which to keep a heifer or a cow, using some poles or rails as bars for a gate.

One day when forest fires were running wildly through the country, this brush corral caught fire and burned swiftly. Mother went out amid the thick smoke to let down the bars and save the heifer by leading her out. After saving the animal soon to become a cow, she heard her boy calling "Mother!" from where the calf had been. About three-and-a-half years old but unable to walk because of weak legs, I had swiftly followed mother on my hands and knees. Mother returned to the burning pen to save her boy from the brushfire where the heifer had been. Little did she then know that he would grow up, go away to school and go out to work for the "King of Kings."

When a baby would die, my father seemed to be the natural leader. He made very simple caskets from white ash which grew on our land. He could plane these rough boards with a big jack plane and my first lessons at carpentry were taking little blocks of wood and sandpaper and sanding the boards after my father had planed them. Later he made adult size caskets. He would put two black iron handles, what I would call handles for a tool chest, on each side. If he had any varnish, he would varnish the front side only.

In those days dishes and fragile things came packed in excelsior, which was shredded wood that looked a lot like shredded wheat biscuits today. With this excelsior the women would make a bed in the casket. Flour in those days came in cloth sacks with heavy printing. After washing, the women would place the sacks in the sun for days to bleach out the lettering. They made dish towels from the sacks, as well as aprons, and they would sew these sacks together and make a lining for dad's homemade caskets, using very small tacks around the top.

In the winter season, green wreaths were used with a ribbon to adorn the casket and in the summertime wild flowers. My father would read from the Bible, say a brief prayer and perhaps talk eight to ten minutes. When the people reached the graveside, he would have all the folk say the Lord's Prayer and then he would read a committal from an old church discipline.

Preachers came through on foot about every three months, consequently, my father had more funerals than the ministers; He was not ordained. Far as I can remember all he had was what was then called an exhorter's license, same as I was first issued in my young days. My father was a much-loved man. If I have ever served any church or community where folk thought half as much of me as they did of my father, I would feel greatly honored and feel that life had been very worthwhile.

I'm often reminded of the fellows fishing. As they were rowing in, one said, "That was a good spot. We should have marked it."

"I did," one of the partners said, "I put an X on the boat."

DEVILISHNESS

As a boy I had a chum, or buddy, by the name of Ray. We played together, stayed in each other's homes for meals, overnight and the like. Ray was a very likeable boy, but was always bragging whenever he had an opportunity to do so . . . you know the type—their horses could pull bigger loads than your horses, their cows gave richer milk than your cows, and on and on it went.

When we were young men, two charming young school-teachers came to our country school. These young ladies always attended church on a Sunday afternoon in the schoolhouse. One Sunday afternoon after church Ray said to me, "I'm going to take Miss Lisk to Bentley to church tonight." I could not see where he had been afforded an opportunity to speak to her after dismissal so I said, "Have you asked her yet?" He said, "No, but I am going to."

Ray got to talking to the preacher and out of pure devilishness, with no interest in a girl I hardly knew, I slipped around and invited her to attend church with me that evening three miles away at Bentley. When I saw Ray terminate his conversation with the preacher I slipped away from the scene but was close enough to hear her reply, "I'm sorry, Ray, but I just promised Alvin." The look I received from my friend would have knocked you off the top of Gibraltar. Not to be defeated, his only recourse was to ask the other teacher.

That night I drove "Queen," the doctor's horse that every fair time was on the racetrack and a most valuable animal. That night there were heavy snowdrifts and the horse stumbled and fell. I spoke to "Queen" but she did not even try to get up. Then it was that Miss Iva Lisk spoke to me and said, "Mr. Doten, did you uncheck the horse?" After I unfastened the checkrein and spoke to "Queen" the second time she tossed her head and was on her feet. (No horse can get up unless first it can throw its head.)

However, this did not solve all the problems. In falling, the horse had broken one of the thills or shafts to the cutter. I had to take the hitching strap and wind the splintered shaft to proceed to church; then I had to unwind it to use the hitching strap to tie up the horse and repeat the action after church and rewind the shaft. When we said "Good night," I remarked, "Well, Iva, a poor beginning makes a good ending." This did not go down too well and for some time I was in the dog house . . . But, believe it or not, we two boys married those two girls.

But long before I married Iva Mae I learned that she had driven a horse four miles to school, harnessed it and cared for it both at home and at school.

The Bay County Fair Commission offered $25.00 to the woman that could harness a horse the quickest, and Iva Mae won the $25.00 one year.

The year before we married she climbed on a mowing machine and mowed 40 acres of hay for her father.

(No wonder she knew that the horse that was down needed to be unchecked before she could get up?)

To bed, to bed, said sleepy head.
Wait awhile, says slow.
Put on the pot, says greedy gut,
Let's eat before we go.

COMMUNITY WITCH

When I was a boy, a woman and her husband moved up from Kentucky. For a number of years they had been coming to Michigan to visit with one particular family near us. Finally they made an arrangement whereby they would trade farms, each leaving furniture, dishes, etc. in their respective homes. When the Michigan family reached the Kentucky home there was not a piece of furniture or a teacup in the place. When the Kentucky folk reached the Michigan home they had the furniture and dishes of both families.

The Kentucky woman who now lived in Michigan went to a good country store. Here for the first time in her life she saw on a shelf a number of white earthenware chambers with handles on them. In her impulsiveness she cried, "Oh, what good milk crocks they'll make. I'll take six of them." The hilarious story of her crudeness became the standard laugh of the community.

This conniving woman from "Old Kentuck" became known as the community demon. She must have been a little more than neurotic because she had mesmerized the whole family into following orders. Her so-called husband was one of these undecided, weak individuals who seemed to enjoy her tyrannical method of manipulation. It was nothing for neighbors to hear fighting, screaming, beatings and yelling down the road as they chased one another. When she finally caught him she whipped him (spanked him), or so she called it. He seemed to need this sort of treatment, for he stayed with her and even defended her from other folk, in his own weak way.

These people had inherited nice apple trees along with their Michigan farm. Like other kids we decided those apples were too good to be left on the trees. This witch either heard us or discovered us in the moonlight. We scampered for the highway. I was the smallest with the shortest legs so I was pigtail in the race to escape! Sensing that I was losing the race with her chasing us with a pitchfork and screaming madly, I dropped into a four-foot ditch. The ditch had about eight inches of black muck and water. I lay low in this mess while this woman with her pitchfork jumped the ditch and took after the other four. Not until I saw her return to the house did I dare emerge from my mud bath and did those four fellows laugh at me. I could care less. I would rather have a bath by myself than a confrontation with that witch. I knew she had taken a pitchfork to her husband's foot not long before. She was angry and hysterical and I was not about to be her next victim.

MONEY WILL BUY

A bed but not sleep;
A book but not brains;
Food but not appetite;
Finery but not beauty;
A house but not a home;
Luxuries but not culture;
Amusement but not happiness;
A crucifix but not a Saviour;
A church but not heaven.

(Unknown)

God cures; the doctor sends the bill. *(French proverb)*

* * *

What would you like most for Christmas? . . .Two more weeks to get ready. *(Central Church Bulletin)*

* * *

One may go wrong in many different ways, but right only in one. *(Aristotle)*

* * *

Someone asked Mark Twain about polygamy, and he said, "That's crazy, no man can serve two masters."

* * *

Get out of Grumble Lane and live on Thanksgiving Street. *(Moody)*

* * *

Hair is a problem with both sexes; with women it's tint; with men, t'ain't. *(Central Church Bulletin)*

* * *

Cooperate. Remember the banana. Every time he leaves the bunch he gets skinned. *(Olive Nold)*

* * *

SMILE—Everybody understands that language. *Unknown*

* * *

The regulations we live under today are something. . . Before long you will have to have permission to kiss your wife.

THREE LIGHTNING BOLTS

Four families went back in the woods and cut out homes. "Old Lou," my dad's old white ox, was the only transportation for the four families. If anything was moved, "Old Lou" had to do the job. He had horns about 15 inches long with a one-inch brass knob on the end. I must have been about nine or ten years old and as usual was out in early evening hunting the cows in a light rain.

All of a sudden out of the breaking clouds came a sharp bolt of lightning and struck a tree about 12 feet ahead of me, going 'round and 'round the tree, stripping off the bark, leaving about a six-inch trail. This tallest tree in the swamp looked more like a barber pole than anything else. I was stunned all over—like one feels when his foot or hand goes to sleep!

When the lightning reached the ground, it tore into a mossy mound and made a big gaping hole. Curiosity pulled me up close to look in the cavity and lo, I spotted a piece of shiny brass. When I picked up the brass, darned if it was not the top of a horn in which little red ants had made a home. I took a stick and pounded until all the ants were out, then carried my trophy home. When my father saw it he said, "Why, that's 'Old Lou's' horn, where on earth did you get it?" After I told my story, mother said, "My boy, thank God," and father said, "I always blamed Butch, but he didn't steal that horn after all. Some dog just carried it away and buried it at the foot of that tall tree."

When I was growing up I worked for a poultry house out Ogden Avenue, West Chicago. Every morning around half-past 10 o'clock I went a couple blocks to the post office for the company mail. This morning I had secured the mail and was angling across this main intersection, under an overhead light with five bulbs where two streetcar power lines crossed. I was perhaps six or eight feet from

being right beneath the spot where these power lines crossed. Lightning struck. For about 10 feet across the world
turned blue right down into the ground! When I came to at
two o'clock in the afternoon I was in the doctor's office
and askéd, "How did I come to be here?"

On my second assignment in the ministry I was sent to
three country churches southwest of Pinconning. The man
that I followed was a very good man assigned to the church
in Pinconning. On the Fourth of July we arranged a joint
meeting for the youth from each church in the form of picnic, program and games at the bay east of town. With my
horse-and-buggy I met my father and mo-
ther at the train at 10 o'clock in the morning. I had just
tied my horse up at the picnic ground, went into the tent
and was drinking a glass of ice-cold lemonade when a blue
flash of lightning went through the tent and the ice-cold
glass I was holding was crushed into hundreds of pieces!
Someone said, "Preacher, you dropped it." I said, "No, I
still have the top of the glass in my fingers," for there I was
holding a half-inch rim of glass!

By now someone shouted, "A man has been struck!"
A few feet away, in line with the tent, lay the man. My
father picked him up by the feet and Reverend Buttler and
I, with our arms under his body, carried him into the tent.

The mortician told us that he took two quarts of clotted
blood from around his heart. Whether the Good Lord was
just trying to shake me up or save me because He had
something left for me to do, I never knew.

There is no use whatever trying to help people who do
not help themselves. You cannot push anyone up a ladder
unless they be willing to climb. *(Andrew Carnegie)*

STOVE POLISH

I had to leave my backwoods township to get to a high school. *When* the day came to go, my father gave me a twenty dollar bill. As he handed me the bill with Andrew Jackson's picture on it, he said, "Laddie, that may do you for six weeks, but it's all I can do." Starting out in the world with a twenty dollar bill and knowing well that father's statement was true, I dreamed of a rather shaky six weeks. Father having cooked for the sheriff in a lumber camp, I secured a room at the courthouse, went to Weaver's hardware and asked for a job to help me go to school.

Tom Weaver was building a new house and gave me the job of picking up after the carpenters after school hours. This netted 50 cents and looked good to me. After a couple of weeks Tom Weaver said, "Kid, you are pretty small, but I have a job you just might handle." The job was one of assembling stoves after school and on Saturdays. Of course, I was assigned the hardest ones first, the cook ranges. In case you have an electric stove, you may very well, after all, wonder just what a kitchen range was? It was a huge iron stove that came out about four feet from the wall and was about five feet long. It had no legs but the whole massive thing went clear down and sat on the floor. It had six griddles on top, any of which you could take out and set in a pot to boil. It had an upright back against the wall with a warming oven about two feet above the stove. The door on this warming section lifted up and disappeared like an old-fashioned rolltop desk. You could keep food warm in this section for latecomers . . . One end of the stove was a reservoir which gave you hot water, providing you did not forget to fill it once a day.

You could only put one stove together each night, and

then black it with stove polish. (This meant a bath every night.)

After two weeks with the ranges out of the way we started in on the heating stoves. We soon learned that, with a little more effort, we could do two of these in an evening and this meant a dollar a day. All this money in a day when men worked *10* hours for $1.25 a day . . . As we came toward the end of the six weeks' run we were down to the small heaters with only four legs to bolt and perhaps a shiny nickel rim to attach and we made up to $4.00 and $4.50 on a Saturday. The 50 cents still helped though the stoves were small.

Evidently the Weavers wanted to help a boy go to school.

After we had been shining stoves for about two weeks, a tall, well-dressed man came in and said to the manager, "Who is the kid working his head off out there?" "That is Bill Doten's kid from out west in the brush. He thinks he wants to go to school." The tall man came back to me and said, "Laddie, do you like horses?" I said, "I just love horses." He asked me half a dozen other questions that I could not put together, then disappeared. In about an hour he returned and said, "I have three very beautiful horses." Then he added, "I just went home and talked with Sarah," whereupon I said, "Well, who is Sarah?" He answered, "Sarah is my wife and I am a doctor. We need somebody to look after the office and our three nice horses and we decided we'd like to have you for our boy." I replied, "I sure would like that, but I promised Mr. Weaver to finish his stoves and I would not want to disappoint him. After the stoves are finished I'd like very much to care for the horses." The Abraham Lincoln-like doctor said, "When you are through with the stoves you come and talk with Sarah and me. Sarah is a lovely woman, everyone else likes her and so will you."

The doctor secured a room for me in an undertaking establishment across the street. You had to go through the mortician's shop to get into their living room.

In those days the caskets were bought very plain and trimmed and lined by the undertaker. He made a bed of excelsior, tacked lace around the inside, etc. This was done on two wooden horses in the workshop.

One night rather late I looked after my horses, then started through the mortician's workshop only to run into a half-lined open casket in the dark, pushing over the horses supporting it and falling head-first into the casket with both arms over the sides, in pain! The owner of the establishment heard the noise, came, and turned on the light.

I can still hear him laughing.

It was not many weeks until the doctor's wife cleaned out the storeroom and made a very good room for the chore boy. They took me to live with them. This was a rare treat and a great inheritance on life's way.

Sarah, the doctor's wife, helped me with my English, which I needed badly and the doctor with my Latin and mathematics.

I soon learned that the doctor's father had been a New England minister and religion ran deep in this home. I will never forget one demand the doctor made of me.

He said, "You were raised a Methodist, but we belong to the Congregational Church. We shall expect you to be in the Methodist Sunday School and church every Sunday except when I am tied up in surgery; then I want you to take my good wife and escort her down the aisle on that red carpet, find the number of the hymn for her and sit with her during service."

Never will I forget that first morning when I walked ahead of Sarah down that aisle on that red carpet escorting her to the second pew from the front which she had requested. I am sure that my ears were redder than the carpet, but we had to learn how to do things somehow.

POPCORN

Ralph, the son of the prosecuting attorney, was about six feet, two inches tall with heavy black hair and I, with my five feet and two inches and blond hair were about as different as any two fellows could be, yet we were nearly always together.

Ralph's father had some half-sash storm windows about three feet square. Ralph and I figured that if we could build a base three feet square and mount it on the wheelbarrow with these half-sash windows upright on three sides, then build a top to cover, we would have the makings of a portable popcorn machine.

We ran a small chain across from the top, allowing enough slack that it would sink about 10 inches in the middle, with the weight of the corn popper operated over a gasoline torch. This established us as novices on the main street of town. We soon did a thriving business for a couple of high school freshmen.

Come the Fourth of July and the town put on quite some program for a County Seat town. They had everything from horseshoes to horse racing, including, of course, a baseball game. They had built a temporary bandstand just west of the bank near the stone depot, over the main street coming into town.

Someone had made a long box to hold something over $300.00 worth of fireworks. This was placed on the bandstand from which, after darkness, the fireworks were to be shot. One of the musicians carelessly threw a cigarette or a cigar stub into the box containing the fireworks. At first they started down Main Street one by one, with their glowing tails! Soon they were coming in groups of rockets, Roman candles and what not?

A man sitting on the bank steps had a rocket go through his hat, another went through a man's arm and broke both bones. By this time the people started coming eastward en masse and they kept coming like a stone wall, only it was a human wall!

I said to Ralph, "Get your head out of the glass!" And immediately the whole homemade popcorn machine was upside down, the wheelbarrow on top and little Alvin with his five foot, two inches standing on top of the upturned wheelbarrow shouting, "Glass! Glass! Look out for the glass!" (Actually, I was not so much concerned about the glass as I was the round paper carton that contained all our change.)

The truth was, we had altogether too much help in picking up our money. *We* were $14 short on the final count. But with all the bad luck on the climax of the Fourth of July celebration, we two fellows each put $60.00 in the bank the next morning.

I've often sat upon a rock content without a meal and often beat the devil down for tempting me to steal. *(Unknown)*

Teacher: What was the Iron Age?
Student: The time before drip dry.
                    (Church Bulletin)

SCRAMBLE FOR YOUR LIFE

When I was 15 I lived with a doctor and took care of his horses. He took me on my first real expedition out into the world. Together we boarded a train at 2:00 o'clock in the morning in Standish, Michigan. By daylight, we were in Detroit. Then we went west on another Michigan Central train to Ann Arbor where I was to see my first major sports event, something different from a sandlot baseball game. It was the fall of the year. The football game was between the University of Wisconsin and the University of Michigan.

The game had progressed into the fourth quarter. We were standing on the bleachers at about the center of this particular section of bleacher seats.

Out of nowhere came the weirdest squeaking sound. The bleachers moved just a little, maybe an inch or two.

The crowd started to surge ahead to get down off the bleachers!!! Firmly the doctor said, "Keep your feet on the plank, boy! Keep your feet right on the plank!" Suddenly the bleachers seemed to shift to the left. Then, they just folded to the ground. The two football teams automatically broke out of formation. They raced to the fences surrounding the stadium. With their strong arms they pulled the wire and heavy posts up out of the ground. These athletes held the heavy posts on their shoulders while the crowd surged through to the field.

The players permitted no hysterics. The game must go on. They just directed us. They really were dividing the crowd and distributing the people all around the edge of the huge playing field. When we were all in position, they resumed the game. Out of a crowd of 2,000 people there was only one accident. This was a broken leg sustained by a doctor from Grayling, Michigan.

50

This particular score was what players call "lopsided," 28 to 0. The game itself wasn't much. An unexpected game, played in the bleachers, provided the excitement that was not forgotten for years.

Instead of scramble for yardage with the football, the game was *scramble for your life!!!*

TOO GOOD FOR THE PRIEST

The first part of my life was spent around lumber camps, sawmill men, tie cutters and woodchoppers. Pat was an Irish woodchopper who lived in a tar paper shanty. One day the Priest came to see Pat. He censured Pat for some of his wayward ways. Noon came and Pat fed him a meal of cornmeal mush. The Priest said, "Pat, you ought not live like this. Is this all you have to eat?"

"Now, Father," said Pat, "if you are a child of God, this is plenty good enough for you, and if you are not a child of God, it is altogether too good."

HALLOWEEN

Chimneys in the early days did not reach the ground. They rested on upright planks about six feet tall. The space between the planks was always used for a closet. One of my Saturday tasks was to do some chores around the doctor's office.

I'll never forget the day I just happened to be in the doctor's office on a Saturday when the cleaning lady was working in the inner office. Planning to clean the closet, if need be, she suddenly jerked aside the green curtain protecting the "under the chimney" closet. She let out a scream that could raise the dead. Immediately she slumped down on the office couch and fainted. I was only a boy, but I knew enough to get something and get it fast. I applied a towel wrung out of cold water. She revived—but she did no more scrubbing that day. For a moment I believe that she thought she, herself, had raised the dead right there in the doctor's office.

The charwoman did not know that this lifelike skeleton remained in the closet under the chimney three months of each year. The other nine months it was in a closet in the health classroom up at the high school.

One year, just before Halloween, some of us decided to have a little fun with that skeleton up at the school. We just wanted people to think that spooks were playing games with them.

First, one of our gang climbed the belfrey and tied a heavy four-foot cord to the bell. To this cord we attached a clothesline which we had just "borrowed" from McRay's yard nearby. We threw the clothesline outside the bell tower to the ground below. We gathered up the line and lay in a popcorn field back of the school. Lying flat on our stomachs in the field we could pull the clothesline and ring the bell in the tower. It was not long before the village firemen were right there. They surrounded the school building but could find nothing. Being volunteers, they returned to their homes.

On the third ringing of the bell the fire department recruited many volunteers. The situation became too alarming for us. We jerked the clothesline very hard. This broke the light cord up close to the bell. We then pulled this clothesline into the popcorn patch, and for all I know, it could be there yet!

About a week before Halloween, five of us had a real good streak. We offered to help the janitor each night after school. In those days the boilers were fired by four-foot cord wood. Because we had been helping the janitor we could easily leave a window unlocked above the wood pile. Thus we could gain access to the schoolhouse. Once inside the school building it was simple to get into the unlocked classroom that held the doctor's skeleton. When Halloween night finally arrived, we scampered up to the top of the woodpile and into the schoolhouse.

In the dark, on the bottom step at the foot of the stairs, we drew cuts to learn who would go up and get the skeleton. Four long matches and one half-match were used. I know now (but I did not know then), that, in the dark the long matches had all been drawn before someone said to me, "Alvin, have you drawn yet?"

Of course I drew the half-match. The other four fellows had it figured out that I lived with the doctor and, therefore, I should be the bravest one to get his "bones."

It is well over 70 years, but I easily remember what I said to that skeleton when I reached up and took him off the hook in the dark. "Come on, you old skeezix, come with me," I muttered as I dragged him down the steps, his toes clattering along in the dark. When I took him through the front door the other four boys ran. I yelled, "You cowards, come back here." Reluctantly, they accepted my challenge to their cowardice.

One of the flag rope snaps was attached to a wire in the skeleton's neck; the other one was snapped to a wire in his knee. Then we ran him up the pole where "Old Glory" should be in the morning. One of the fellows who could shimmy up a pole climbed up about 30 feet and wound the flag rope around the pole. Then he slipped down.

In the morning, at least 200 people, in addition to the school pupils, gathered to see "Old Bones" in place of the flag. At last, after all the excitement, the fire department was called to bring their ladders and get "Old Bones" down.

It wasn't long before Mr. McCarty, Secretary of the School Board, a man whose office was above the bank, called me up into his office and said, "Alvin, you come from a good family out West. We need your help in determining who put the skeleton up the flagpole Halloween night. That kind of thing cannot be permitted to just happen. Keep your ears open and see what you can learn and let me know."

Two weeks later the secretary called the doctor with whom I lived and had him send me up to his office. Of course, I had not learned a thing. These trips were repeated for six weeks. The pressure was getting to all five of us. It had become common knowledge, that these boys, whoever they were, were headed for the reform school. The Secretary of the School Board placed an ad in the newspaper: "$50.00 reward for information leading to any boy who helped put the skeleton up the flagpole."

One night after supper, the doctor said to me, "Alvin, I have a hunch that you know more about my skeleton than any of the other boys. I just believe you were in on that Halloween prank. If you were, tell me about it. I believe I can help you out."

It did not take me long to tell the whole story. I had wanted to unwind about it for a long time. The doctor then said, "Well, I was right. Tell you what I want you to do. You go up to Mr. McCarty's office and tell him that you have some news for him. Tell him that you were one of the boys and that you will tell the school board, at their next meeting Monday night, who all of the other boys are."

Monday night arrived. The meeting was called to order. The minutes of the previous meeting were read and

54

accepted. The doctor had requested time to speak to the school board. He began by saying, "I think you fellows are making a mountain out of a mole hill. These boys didn't take any wheels off from any buggies. They didn't push over any water closets. They didn't break anything. They just had some good clean fun with my skeleton, and they didn't hurt him a bit." Then he added, "Alvin, why don't you tell the school board members who the boys were?"

I came out with, "Well, to begin with, one was 'Reddy' Carpenter, the redheaded printer's devil who helped in the town newspaper office after school. One was Bill Forsyth, the mayor's boy; Hank Poweroy, the sheriff's son; six-foot and black-haired Ralph Hayes, the prosecuting attorney's boy, and, then there was me."

I can still hear that doctor saying, "If I were the secretary of this school board and a senator down at the state capitol, I don't think I'd stir this pot. You're going to be dealing with the mayor's boy, the sheriff's son and the prosecuting attorney's boy. I think I'd just forget the whole thing."

And we never heard another word about the skeleton's journey heavenward.

A little girl said to a boy in Sunday School, "Why do they say *AMEN* in church instead of *A WOMAN*?"

The boy answered back, "I'm sure I do not know unless it's because they sing hymns instead of hers."
(Methodist Bulletin)

LESSONS IN SURGERY

One of the initial experiences in the care of a doctor's office was something very dramatic which had nothing to do with the care of the office—rather with the emergency care of a patient.

One Saturday morning a railway brakeman had his hand caught on coupling pins between the box cars. The man was rushed into the doctor's office. No nurse was there at the moment. I was helping clean up the office. The doctor turned to me and said, "Here, boy, hold this man's hand while I cut off his four fingers." As a rule I do not perspire, but I surely did that day. When the doctor finished, the brakeman had only a thumb on his right hand.

Next, the doctor told me to go bury the fingers out by the woodpile. I was about as 'scaird' of these fingers as I would have been of a corpse. I did not take the time to bury them very deep.

In less than an hour a dog showed up in a bar room, downtown, with a man's finger in his mouth. (The rumors of murder went all over the town.) Alvin was in for his first serious trouble. With a scrap bone from the butcher shop we retrieved the finger from the big dog. This time we buried it deep—at least three feet with four stones on top before we filled the hole.

This was not my only experience in helping to care for the doctor's patients. This man, Dr. Toothaker (he should have been a dentist), was of good New England stock. He was a graduate of Massachusetts Medical, Johns Hopkins and Ann Arbor. He was well equipped and a clever surgeon. He did not give up easily. He taught me how to shape a newspaper into a cowbell, pin light towels around and inside of it, sprinkle in chloroform, and use it to put patients to sleep.

One thing led to another. Before long I was getting up at four o'clock in the morning, feeding a horse while the maid got my breakfast. By five o'clock the horse and I were on our way. It might be four miles; it might be fifteen miles to the home where they needed a doctor. As soon as we arrived we would ask the folks to build a big fire in their old kitchen range. Next we asked for their clothes boiler. After we scrubbed the boiler, we placed the instruments in a cheesecloth bag and boiled them on the range. This was sterilization, if you please.

After eating, again, with the family we had them clear the dining room table. I prepared the table by placing three-inch pads on it. Then we awaited the doctor's arrival. He would not vary ten minutes—one way or the other—from eight o'clock. We had our paper covered cowbell ready, sprinkled in the chloroform and put the patient to sleep in preparation for the doctor's role as surgeon.

In those days, the doctor collected about 60% of his accounts. Whether he received his pay or not, I always got $5. The doctor always saw to it that I was back in school by one o'clock in the afternoon. The teachers never said a word to Alvin. They all seemed to know what was going on and wanted to lend a helping hand. There was never any calling on the carpet for truancy and somehow we always seemed to pass the examinations.

As I look back now to those days, I can sense that if the doctor was able to send a nurse to the home for a couple of weeks following surgery, the patient usually survived. If the family could not afford a nurse; or, if no nurse was available, the patient often expired—in spite of the surgery.

Just before I was 15 I had seen a baby come into the world. Evidently, someone had a plan for my life.

After a lot of such coaching, the doctor said, "You have small hands. You'll make a really fine surgeon."

(This wonderful man offered to see me through medical school.) I came back with, "But, I don't want to be a surgeon. I want to be a preacher man."

I will never forget his final answer, "Alvin, I hope that you get enough to eat."

CHILDHOOD MEMORIES

Air: Tramp, tramp, tramp, the boys are marching.

O, the little busy bee, in the garden you may see,
    Gathering honey thro' the golden summer hours,
He is cheery and he's gay, and intent he works away
    Storing treasures from the sweetly blooming flowers.

Chorus: Working, working in the sunbeams
    Gathering honey all the day,
O, the little busy bee is the type for you and me,
    For the winter he provides in sunny May.

(Knapsack)

Around the house this doctor was always singing some crazy song. I suppose it was release from the pressures of surgery. The following is an example.

TRAVELLING

A young man went to see his girl
    One dark and stormy night;
He asked her if she'd be his wife
    He thought 'twould be alright.
Her father said "You're wrong my boy
    You'll go right home instead."
And Harry went travelling, travelling
    Back to the old folks at home.

At Saratoga once I went
    To see the ponies race
A friend said "You play Bumblebee
    He's sure to win a place"
On Bumblebee I put my pile,
    But as the race was won
He stopped to buzz around awhile
    And I got badly stung.
So Harry went travelling, travelling
    Back to the old folks at home.

A thousand men once tried to pull
    A mule from off the track.
They pulled him just about a foot
    And then he pulled them back.
Then someone did a funny thing
    He must have been a fool.
He went and got a piece of straw
    And tried to tickle that mule.
And Harry went travelling, travelling
    Far from the old folks at home.

STRANGE BEDFELLOWS

When I was in my teens I found myself, through a friendship with a doctor who was interested in a plant on the west side of Chicago, working for a poultry concern. This company had a number of thousands of pairs of mated pigeons. My duties included working in the plant two days each week where we fed and dressed the squabs or baby pigeons and when they were 28 days old, we broke their necks and dry picked them for the market. Two days of the week were spent purchasing grain. The other two were spent selling poultry to the leading hotels and restaurants in downtown Chicago. Only the best of the gourmet restaurants and hotels were our customers.

I would often buy one dozen overripe bananas. I would eat about four of them for lunch and give the remaining bananas to a group of waiting urchins who readily devoured them.

Although I usually had enough for lunch and transportation I found myself stranded one day in downtown Chicago without a nickel. This carelessness was one of my first lessons in resourcefulness. I had to work my own way out of this predicament. No one in the "Loop" cared or would share his money with me.

I thought a while and decided to go directly to the buyer of food for the Congress Hotel on Michigan Avenue. Two hours earlier I had sold this man a good order of birds. As a rule these hotels paid two weeks later. I explained my predicament to the buyer and he said, "There's an easy way around that one, I'll just give you a voucher for $60.00 that would be due in two weeks." Thus it was I had money for lunch and streetcar fare home because he trusted me and admired my courage in coming to him for a business advance.

Our hired help at this plant was mostly very young, some under 17 years of age. Young as I was, only 18, I was considered foreman. One day I hired a Negro boy by the name of George Proctor. The other boys left nothing undone that would nettle George. We all slept in a large type of open bedroom on the third floor in a large home on the west side of Chicago in what was known as the Morton Park area.

One night the boys carried their harassing to an extreme degree of behavior. I called George to my bed and said, "George, get your pillow and sleep with me tonight." He couldn't believe what I was telling him. "I mean it, George, get your pillow and come with me."

After three nights of sleeping with me, I said, "George, try your own bed tonight." John Daly, the tough leader among the help, said to me after George returned to his own bed, "Are you really going to keep George Proctor here working with us?" I replied, "George will be the last one to go!!" From that moment on, I never had another moment's trouble with the help.

I don't know what happened to the other boys, but George Proctor made a real contribution to the world. He studied medicine with his nurse-wife and they spent their lives in Africa helping people who needed their medical knowledge.

It has been a comforting memory through the years to think about George. Sleeping with George three nights did something for George, but more for Alvin and for the world.

One ought every day at least to hear a little song, read a good poem, see a fine picture, if it were possible, to speak a few reasonable words. *(Johann W. Goethe)*

FIRST CONFERENCE

I started preaching the last Sunday in June, 1909, taught school and preached to the Indians. In early September, 1910, we took an interurban car from Saginaw to Detroit. The tracks for the interurbans followed pretty much the contour of the land. When you were going up-hill, it was all right, but they traveled at high speed and as they dropped swiftly down in the valleys you held on to your stomach, ofttimes with both hands. At Flint a young man came into the coach and took the seat right in front of me. He immediately began reading a book entitled *Prophecy and the Prophets*. Having just studied that same book, I was certain he was bound for conference. I was too reticent to say, "Brother, you must be going to conference?"

At that time, Detroit, to me, was the metropolis of the world and I had not the faintest idea of where to get off that car, but I decided that when that little man ahead of me alighted, I would follow very close by. All of a sudden he quickly closed his book and took his small case and I followed. Soon the interurban pulled away and there across the street stood Central Church, the first cathedral I had ever seen. The young man walked into the church office and, registered as Frank Field, was assigned a home in which to stay. I walked up and said, "I am Alvin Doten," and I was also assigned a home for lodging and breakfast. Frank Field later started Oak Park Church, of Flint, by holding services in a tent in an old apple orchard. Frank Field went on to become a man of tremendous leadership in Methodism. Once, when I became discouraged on life's road, this same Frank Field put his arm around me and knelt on the carpet of his district parsonage home and gave me the courage to go on.

Bishop McDowell of Washington was the presiding Bishop of this Conference and the first Bishop I had ever seen. He preached on "A Sower Went Forth to Sow" and described his father with bags of wheat on a dray drawn by an ox. I could see my father with his big white ox called "Old Lou," slowly plodding to a new field, drawing a dray loaded with bags of wheat for seed and little me sitting atop the wheat and to this day that was the greatest sermon I ever heard, "A Sower Went Forth to Sow."

HOW A LAWYER WOULD GIVE YOU AN APPLE

"I hereby give and convey to you, all and singular, my estate and interest, rights, title, claim and advantages with full power to bite, cut and otherwise eat the same, or give the same away with or without the peel, juice, pulp or seeds, anything here before or here-in-after or in any other deed, or deeds, instruments of whatever nature or kind whatsoever to the contrary in anything not withstanding." *(Unknown)*

CALAMITY AT CALUMET

When I was a young minister serving three country churches southwest of Pinconning, Michigan, we were staggered by the newspaper reports of a calamity at Calumet. Little did I think then that the day would come when I would be serving the church at Lake Linden four miles from Calumet and hear this story over and over again and again.

There had been a long bitter strike in the copper industry. It was Christmastime and the folk wanted to do something for the children so they had a mass meeting on Christmas Eve of 1913, in the Italian Hall. This was to be a Christmas celebration to help children forget the hardship of the strike. The union, it is said, had required people attending the party to show some form of identification.

Some 400 persons were assembled in this Italian Hall, making merry in the Christmas party, and the children were big-eyed with anticipation as they watched the gifts and decorations on the tree, when some drunk must have seen a candle flickering and shouted, *"Fire!"* This diabolic cry was then echoed in several languages. One woman, who claimed she had shaken the man who gave this fiendish cry, dashed to the platform to the piano to play in an attempt to calm the crowd! Whatever the argument about the alarmist, no one could deny the devastating results.

The doors to the building opened inward and the panicking people jammed against these doors causing those who had reached there first to suffocate and the stampede continued until 61 children and 11 adults died in this calamity!

Most of the victims were buried in a cemetery outside of Red Jacket. The hymns, "Rock of Ages" and "Nearer My God to Thee" were sung. The services were held in

English, Croatian, Slovenian and Finnish. The pall that fell over so many of the miners' families of different nationalities hung like a heavy cloud in so many homes for many years. It was often spoken of as "Calamity at Calumet." The Italian Hall where this disaster occurred still stands today on Seventh Street in Calumet.

Two factors one would never forget about this country was that the red sandstone used in building came down from the quarry to Lake Linden by gravity, there being a drop of 580 feet from Calumet to Lake Linden.

The other was that while we lived in Lake Linden, four miles away, we learned a new way of life that was very trying until it became a part of you. While the copper rock was mined on the range it was brought down to the stamp mills at Lake Linden for crushing. If I remember correctly there was a battery of 28 steel heads, each about four feet square, which were lifted and dropped to crush the rock. These heads were timed so they did not all drop at the same time so there was continuous crushing and likewise continuous vibration. This heavy machinery made the town quiver a mile away. Dishes jiggled off the kitchen range, pictures on the wall went askew every day, even the bed quivered! Sometimes it would put you to sleep and sometimes it would keep you awake, but you learned to live with this vibration.

This went on 24 hours each day except Sunday when the stamps were quiet for an eight-hour shift and it seemed almost like a funeral.

Dr. Allen Rice came to give a lecture in our church and he began by saying, "This is the only town in my life I was ever in where the whole town had St. Vitus' Dance!"

It is better to go fishing with your boy today than to need to go hunting for him tomorrow. *(Western Livestock Reporter)*

LOST CHILD

One evening a little "tow-headed" girl named Jean did not show up for the evening meal in the home of our local merchant and postmaster. Groups of men were organized to search the river, the creeks, meadows, clumps of bushes, everywhere. The little girl had been missing since very early evening. By dark, even, they frantically hunted on. Finally everyone was exhausted and frustrated. Where was there a place they had not looked?

Long after midnight her mother went upstairs to throw herself down on Jean's bed in anguish. There she found her little child fast asleep.

We lived to see this girl grow up very close to us. It was after her father died, suddenly, that we took her home to live with us. Years later when she was just a young girl, not even in her teens, she revealed her imagination and resourcefulness. She cut a section out of the side of an old vinegar barrel. Next she placed a low soap box, just big enough to sit in, inside of the barrel. Then she paddled it up and down Thunder Bay River, with her hands. Her balancing power was unequaled. All the boys who tried it got a ducking in the water.

Jean went with us on her first trout fishing expedition. When the fish took her bait she landed it on the top of a spruce tree. (She never ceased to hear how she dried her fish up a tree.)

Jean became a very good driver of our car and could even change a tire faster than the preacher. She finally graduated from Marquette High School. After the graduation I found her in the porch swing crying and said, "Jean, what are you 'bawling' about? This should be the happiest day of your life."

"I don't want to leave home," she replied.

"I thought you wanted to be a nurse. I have spoken at the chapel in the Bronson Methodist Hospital, in Kalamazoo, a couple of times. I have made the arrangements for your entrance this fall."

"Oh, dad, you would do that!" were her heartwarming words.

After she was graduated from Bronson as a registered nurse, her first nursing position was in Astoria, Oregon, near the mouth of the Columbia River. Later she returned to graduate school. After training she became an anesthetist.

Calmly and with dignity she served the sick. Efficiently she assisted the doctors and surgeons. Jean was and is a beautiful person. We never helped anyone, on life's way, who was more appreciative. She has been so good to our family.

What is greater than an investment in helping others?

"Inasmuch as ye have done it unto one of the least of these my brethren, ye have done it unto me."

As I grew up my father had a standing deal with me. For every thrashing I received in school, there would definitely be another one at home. This happened just once; that was enough.

CONGREGATION OF TWO

Back in 1912, when I was a young preacher serving three country churches, one Sunday, in particular, stands out . . .

It was a stormy Sunday afternoon when I was preaching at the Garfield Methodist Church, in Bay County, Michigan.

The total congregation was composed of a man and his wife who had driven with a horse-and-cutter through the storm to church. This couple sat on two chairs by the big round wood-burning stove.

The little preacher stood by the same stove and preached a 20 minute sermon directly to them.

About six weeks after this occasion they got a divorce (I doubt that it could have been much of a sermon.)

This reminds me of Walter Brooks, a good-looking minister who always talked too long and too much. At every conference session he would have the "floor" at least a dozen times a day asking some ridiculous question.

I remember once when Reverend Brooks said, "Bishop, what do you think of a man, on a three or four-point circuit, who preaches the same sermon in each church?"

I can see Bishop Blake's twinkle even now. He thought a moment, then said, "Brother Brooks, I think it would be a very poor sermon that wouldn't bear repeating."

This was the end of Walter Brooks. He actually sat down for the rest of the day!

THREE GALLONS OF MILK

Preachers sometimes move by the powers that be and sometimes they move between times. If you are lucky a congregation asks for you. This time we were fortunate indeed; we were moving into a mining town. The problem was a noisy one. Moving 300 miles with a pair of nine-month-old twins is no Sunday School picnic!

We made this move by train. We were scheduled to get off a "Soo" line train at 11:00 o'clock at night and wait for the 9:00 o'clock train in the morning. We had written the young resident minister at the junction, asking him to have a little milk for the babies (our doubleheader twins). As the train ground to a stop, we descended the steps in the night. There was the young preacher saying, "I have the milk alright. I have three gallons."

Then we were confronted with the problem of getting the twins to sleep without their own little basket beds. After an hour of fruitless effort, we emptied two small dresser drawers and tucked them away, like Moses, in their basket-like beds, covered them up and watched. In just eight minutes they were fast asleep.

The patient was coming to after surgery. "Where am I, in Heaven?"

"No, dear," his wife soothed, "you're down here with me." *(Modern Maturity)*

OJIBWAYS

When I was old enough to teach school, the district superintendent sent me to preach to the Frost Lake Indians. As he did so he said, "Alvin, if you stay there until next conference time you will stay any place that the Methodist Church ever sends you."

I remember so well how the superintendent, the Reverend Lewis N. Moon (who later married Iva M. Lisk and me), said, "Alvin, when you go to the Indians the first time you will know before you come away whether or not you go a second time. You can tell by where they tell you to sleep. The chief's house is made of hewn logs. You stay with the chief's family. If they make your bed on the floor, you get up the next morning and just forget all about them. This means that they have not accepted you. If they give you their bed, the only bed that they have, and they sleep on the floor, then you will know that you have been accepted. You can go back the next Saturday, and spend the Sabbath with them again."

On the first Saturday that I went in to visit these Frost Lake Indians I went directly to the hewn log house because the chief would naturally be the leader of the "band." I knocked on the door but no one answered. I thought that I heard some kind of a commotion from up above; so, I stepped back and looked up at the roof. The entire ridge was lined with Indian heads with just the eyes and the top of their heads showing. There must have been 20 of them but as soon as they caught my eyes they were gone, simultaneously, it seemed.

I went around behind the house. One Indian was peeking out from behind a tree. Another had dropped down into the rain barrel. I saw four of them in two canoes that were out on the lake. All the rest had just disappeared. I turned to the one Indian, nearby, the one in the rain barrel.

"Where are all the folks?" I asked. "Berry-picking," was his answer. Some of the Indians nearby were anxious about the lone Indian in the barrel. They started coming out from behind bushes and trees. Soon I had all of them there except for four who got away in the canoes. I told them stories and asked them questions. Finally, the older folks returned with the cleanest, hand-picked blueberries that you ever saw.

That night, when it came time to retire, by luck they offered me their bed. Finally they decided that I just did not know how to go to bed. The chief lighted a lantern, said something to his wife and they both went out into the darkness of the night. If ever anyone went to bed in a hurry, it was I. They returned. Using a short ladder they took down a mattress from some overhead poles. They placed it right up against my bed. This way I could not possibly get out without stepping right on them. Then they proceeded to throw a blanket over their heads and undress. (I had just learned how to get myself ready for bed.)

In the morning I heard some "jibbering" in Ojibway. Next I saw a big brown arm come out from under a blanket and get a stocking. Next the arm came out and picked up another article. Soon they were dressed. The mattresses were put up above. Immediately, I put a blanket over my head and proceeded to get dressed.

We had pancakes and blueberries for breakfast. About 10 o'clock approximately 30 Indians gathered in that home for the Sunday service. The hymns were all sung in the "Chippewa Tongue." When it was time for my short sermon I would talk about three minutes, then the chief would interpret the words to the Indian folk. Then I talked another three minutes, my round. His followed. This went on until I had used up about 25 minutes. We sang a couple more hymns in Ojibway (the Indian term for Chippewa). After church we had a wonderful fish feed. This was served out of doors, on long tables. All of the Indian families participated. Blueberries and brown sugar was the dessert.

Some Sunday mornings I would speak briefly—then we would have an all around testimonial meeting. All of the Indians, except the chief and his assistant, would speak in their tongue. I will never forget how one morning the assistant to the chief, my interpreter and Indian local preacher, Moses (Wosh-Tah-Yan) Smith, spoke in English. He blurted out, "Preacher, you like him apple pie, lots of sugar, some cinnamon on him, good and spicy." Then he added, "That am Jesus Christ to me. He am the spice of life." Then he sat down. He had preached quite a sermon.

One Saturday, the superintendent of our church came north with me, on the train, to West Branch, Michigan, to the Indian service. The minister, in his buggy, met us. He had a basket of fried chicken and a jar of green tea. I drove the horse while the superintendent ate. Then he drove while I ate. I will never forget when he took the first swig out of that jar of green tea. He said, "My goodness, it is strong enough to raise the dead."

The superintendent and I, of course, drew the bed; while the chief and his wife slept on the floor. This was to be the big day of the year with Dr. Moon, the preacher-man. We had planned a communion after the morning service. I had asked the Indians to prepare some blueberry juice to use for communion wine. When the superintendent served me, he then took a taste of the wine. He whispered to me, "My goodness, it has the 'old stick' in it." I answered, "Use it or we will be all done here." Afterward I explained how the assistant to the chief had walked eleven miles (22 miles round trip) to get a little whiskey to put in the berry juice.

Not long afterward this assistant walked me a long way to see something that he wanted much for the preacher to see. It was a spring on the side of a hill. It bubbled out and formed a stream about 10 inches wide. This cascaded down the grade. This Indian man had built a set of earthen steps, cut out of clay. He did this so he could go to the top and look down on the cascading stream, from the spring. When he took me to this quiet spot was the time I chose to tell him that the next time we had communion he need not walk the 22 miles to get the liquor. We would just use the blueberry juice, plain!

One evening an Indian squaw tried to feed me fried snake for supper and I said, "Oh, no! I have eaten your raccoon, your porcupine, your squirrels and your sweet muskrat meat; but, I will not eat your snake!"

She replied, "You had him, for dinner. *Soup.*"

(By the way, if you run out of food in the woods, just dig up some cattail roots and boil them and you will have pretty good potatoes. Here's hoping you have some salt? And the tender tops of the young cattails make splendid greens.)

I learned many practical things from the Indians. One thing I learned was that if you put your small hand of your watch or wrist watch on the sun and count backwards half way around to twelve from the little hand, it will be "North," every time. Another practical bit of knowledge that I learned from the Indians is that moss grows only on the north side of a tree . . . They taught me that if you take a very small piece of wood, the size of a toothpick, and stand it on your thumbnail you will always get a shadow. If you know anything at all about where the shadows fall, at that time of day, you can very easily ascertain which direction is north.

If you are out in the woods you can break a wee end of a twig off a branch and stand it on your thumbnail. Immediately you get your shadow—even in a rainstorm.

Perhaps your partner went on a trail into a camp a day ahead of you. You were to follow the morrow. If you came to a place where the trail divided, you would discover that your partner, the Indian, had broken a twig, about eight inches long, and left it hanging down so that you would know which way to go. You were to break it off and drop it to the ground so as not to fool or confuse anyone else who might come along that way. The Indians had so many simple tricks for the woodsman!

I remember an outstanding Indian who one morning in a class meeting said, "I have something in here," pointing to his heart. "When I do wrong it turns around

INDIAN PRAYER

GREAT SPIRIT –

GRANT THAT I
MAY NOT CRITICIZE MY
NEIGHBOR UNTIL I HAVE
WALKED FOR A MOON IN
HIS MOCCASINS

THE SIOUX VERSION

and it has points on it and the points really hurt, but if you do wrong too much of the time the points wear off and they don't seem to hurt anymore." Then he added, "That is conscience."

Some of the better class of Indians built grave houses over the graves of their loved ones. These houses were two-and-one-half to three feet high and would originally be constructed of bark. As the bark decayed, they cheapened the job with the white man's lumber, but they always perpetuated the chieftain's grave house in bark.

The Indians always left an opening in the end of each grave house about 5" x 10" in size, through which, on the anniversary of their deaths they could feed the spirits of the departed. They placed in the opening bread and whiskey. The birds of the air took the bread and the boys skipped school to get the whiskey, so it was, the spirits accepted their offerings.

West of Crystal Falls in the Upper Peninsula you will find one of these burying grounds with the grave houses and the openings through which you can feed the spirits.

When approached by his minister for a contribution, the miser protested, "I thought salvation was free."

The preacher replied, "It is, my friend, and so is water, but you have to pay for having it piped to you." *(Unknown)*

INDIAN GRAVE HOUSES

INDIAN HERITAGE

Alcona	Beautiful Plain
Alpena	Partridge
Ameek	Beaver
Chessaning	Big Rock
Chicagon	Lake Skunk Place
Chickaming	Lake
Copemish	Big Beech
Escanaba	Land of the Red Deer
Gegaming	Porcupine
Geguac	Pleasant Water
Ishpeming	Heaven
Leelanau	Land of Delight
Macatawa	Black Lake
Mahepac	Pine Forest
Manitou	Great Spirit
Manistee	Spirit of the Woods
Manistique	Vermillion
Menominee	Wild Rice
Munising	Island in Lake
Muskegon	Marshy River
Millecoquins	Plenty Hardwoods
Nunica	Clay Earth
Naubinawa	Place of Echoes
Nahma	Sturgeon
Neebish	Water Boils
Nekema	Fishing Grounds
Nebesshone	Bend in River
Niles	Running Water
Ogemaw	Chief
Ogenta	Pickerel
Omena	It Is So
Ocqueec	Crooked Waters
Oscoda	Pebbly Prairie

Oshtemo	Head Waters
Ontonnagon	Bowl
Pewabic	Mineral Section
Pequaming	Paradise
Petoskey	Rising Sun
Pinconning	Little Potatoes
Quanicacce	Lone Tree
Quinnesec	Smoky Waters
Sidnaw	Little Hill by Creek
Sagola	Welcome
Saugatuck	Mouth of River
Sebewaing	Crooked Creek
Saginaw	Place of the Sauks
Siskiwit	Lake Trout
Keweenaw	Portage
Keneckee	Long Legged
Kalamazoo	Mirror or Reflection in Water

We are a generation of technical contradictions. We can send men and machines to the moon, we can blow the world to bits in a matter of minutes, but we cannot feed one-third of the world's people who are malnourished. *(Harry Haines)*

KEEN COMPETITION

In 1911 the Bishop moved us from Midland Circuit to Pinconning Circuit. (By the way, "Pinconning" is the Indian word for "little potatoes.") The parsonage was located about nine miles southwest of Pinconning. It was a small brick house beside the Fraser church. There was a town hall and a store operated by a man named "Tanner." There was a long string of buggy sheds for the horses in bad weather. The schoolteacher was a widow with a little girl with long brown curls and they boarded with us in the parsonage home.

One of the great events of each year was the Fraser picnic held in John Shoe's woods. Folks came from far and near. We always had some outstanding speaker as well as games galore. I remember one year we scheduled a preacher's wrestling match. Though I was small, I was very quick and "believe it or not" I won that wrestling match!

Another point about the Fraser picnic was that we always had a case of lemons for lemonade. This year we had half a case left, so the preacher cut them in halves and sold them along with a stick of candy for a dime. You would suck the juice of the lemon through the porous candy and it was delicious!

Soon folks were excited and afraid they were not going to get half a lemon and a candy stick and they began offering 25¢ a piece! In no time we had only the empty lemon crate. Folks said, "Watch your clothes, or the preacher will sell them!"

In this Fraser church there was a man named Charlie Bachman. He belonged to the Mennonite faith, but for a couple of Sundays when he was attending their annual meeting he was always in our church, and how Charlie liked to sing! He was always and forever bringing the preacher something to eat. It might be corn, it might be a sack of flour or it might be meat, but he was the great parsonage provider on that job.

While on this field, we "married" Mark Princing's daughter. I remember well that her father drove us 30 miles to Bay City to a photographer. It was in an early vintage Buick and this was some expedition for those years. The couple who stood with the bride and groom that day very soon became Mr. and Mrs. Heppner.

I well remember one November night after church at Bertie. On the northwest corner of the four-mile square was a unique chapel. We started home four miles south and four miles east. A big wind was blowing from the northwest. It was terrific and kept blowing the buggy sidewise to the east! Billy, the horse, would just stop and hump his back until the wind ceased a little. This night of the big wind, 28 boats were lost on the Great Lakes, mostly on Lake Superior. They were mostly barges loaded with lumber. Two or three were ore carriers.

The Bertie church on the northwest of the square was located in a community where all but two families were related. The David Bryce family was the outstanding leader. David Bryce was the "Ezra" of men in that region. His daughter, Lizzie, played the church organ. John Bryce, the older boy, was a rock of Gibraltar.

I remember one Sunday evening after church we drove young Billy Bryce (who was church treasurer) to the Detroit and Mackinaw railway station to bid him farewell as he went off to World War I.

Billy Bryce was blown to pieces in Flanders. This was not easy to live with because Billy had so much potential. But it is the price war demands. In the end everybody loses.

It was in this community that a teacher came to live with the Bryce family. The teacher and John could not keep their eyes off each other so they, too, were married and became a great Kingdom team.

On this charge, Fraser, where the parsonage was located, had service in the morning for three months, then they would revert to evening service and Bertie would have the morning hour of worship. In one span while Bertie was enjoying the morning hour, two fly-by-night preachers came into the community and found favor with the Lowell Grants who lived a couple miles west of the church.

These new preachers would hold services in the homes, but finally persuaded the trustees to allow them to use the church in the evening. They started off by saying that all one had to do to be a preacher in those days was to wear a cutaway coat and a cross on his watch chain! (In those days you wore a cutaway coat and striped trousers.)

This did not go down too well with the loyal church people, but before the week was done, Grandmother Lowell, who lived in Lowell Grant's home, died (leaving 64 great-grandchildren). When the Grants stepped to the telephone to call their preacher man to care for Grandma's funeral, the two fly-by-night preachers packed up and were on their way!

Thus ended some rough competition in our early days.

This was Grandma Lowell's Easter morning and I well remember we closed by singing, "It Is Well With My Soul."

I could never understand how a red cow eats green grass and gives white milk. . . .Many things in God's plan I can't understand, but still I trust Him.

SANATORIUM

Late in the winter of 1916, I did, as they said, "cough my head off." Following the analysis of several sputum samples the laboratory diagnosis came back in one word, "Tuberculosis."

My doctor then made an appointment for me to be examined at the sanatorium in Howell, Michigan. I took a train to Howell but I had to be met by a local bus driver who would drive me the additional five miles to the sanatorium.

Once there, I was examined by a Dr. Toan and re-examined by the superintendent of the sanatorium, Dr. Pierce. When he finished he looked at me and said, "You are the fifth man within the last few hours to be given a diagnosis of tuberculosis. Our problem is one of logistics. We have only one bed. I feel that your prognosis is the best of the five. I also believe that you will be worth more to the world than the other four. The one bed that we do have is yours." (This is once when it paid to be a preacher.)

At the sanatorium, life was scheduled, disciplined and, in a way, rugged. We were always in bed at eight each night. The beds were not in a steam, oil or electric heated room. We slept practically out of doors, in shacks. Each shack had a small lobby, a floor, a roof over much but not all of the area and only canvas storm curtains at the window openings in the wall. The windows were always open. The canvas curtains were closed only if the inclement weather was blowing rain or snow into the shack.

The beds were Klondike style—a little like today's sleeping bags but without the side zipper opening. You slipped down into the bed from the top. To keep warm we had to use earthen crocks about 14 inches in diameter, rounded on top. We *had* to *keep warm* by *using* these crocks, which we affectionately called "pigs." When we snuggled down into the bed we had to work the crock down into the "sack bed" near the bottom. The crock looked like a cut pumpkin with a lid on top. It also had a heavy handle on one side, to which was attached a strong string. The crock kept the bed warm all night. We kept warm by sleeping in a stocking cap and mittens. When morning came and we crawled out we had to take the "crock pot" out also. When we pulled the string we would find that the water in the pot was still warm enough to shave with.

Not all but most of us were ambulatory patients strong enough to dress daily and go to our meals. Each meal demanded that we report—just before the meal—to the infirmary or medical dispensary for our medication. In addition to this, twice a week, a doctor went over your chest very, very thoroughly. We called it "the fine-tooth comb job."

After three months my doctor told me, "Preacher, you are doing well." After six months had passed he told me, "Alvin, your tuberculosis is temporarily arrested." I very quickly learned that his diagnosis was not a release from the confinement of the sanatorium. I was called into the superintendent's office.

"I'd like to make a deal with you," Dr. Pierce said. "With your small frame and slight stature and all your drive and ambition I do not want to release you yet. You will just go out and break yourself down again. Here is what I wish for you to do. Stay here another six months— at no cost to you! You can be a House Father for the boy patients in Heart's Desire Cottage. You will see that they get their temperature taken regularly, take their medication, get to meals on time, to bed on time in the evening and take their two hour afternoon rest. You will not only be helping these young boys, but you will also be writing your own health and life insurance policy."

When a wise doctor presented it to me in this way there was not much of a decision to make. I just looked ahead to the future and stayed there as a preparation for my future life.

As long as I live I will never forget one of the boys in my cabin. His name was Benny Winewski. He was from Grand Rapids, Michigan. Benny was a "stand-up comedian," a circus all by himself. He had such an optimistic outlook on life that this helped him become cured. (Some of the boys were not that fortunate!)

I will always appreciate that from the beginning of my excursion into sanatorium life my good wife, Iva Mae, had been with me. She had chosen to come there and work. She had been there only a short while when they learned of her ability to cut, create patterns and teach the art of sewing. She was immediately made supervisor of the sewing department, at least of one of them.

A nurse by the name of Koblinski and her nine girls, along with my nine cabin boys, occupied one long dining room table. My good wife was given the opportunity to serve food to this particular table. Thus it was that Iva and I got to see and talk to each other at least three times each day.

During these final six months a lady patient, Mrs. Tasker, and I operated a fine Sunday School for all patients who were able to attend.

So it was that I spent one full year institutionalized in a sanatorium. On the 16th of April, 1916, I entered. My discharge date was April 17th, 1917, one year and a day.

Long before my dismissal due date I had ordered a Model "T" Ford Touring car. This new "toy" was ready and waiting for me when I was given those dismissal papers stamped, "Completely arrested case."

I remember realizing that being an "X-lunger," as we called it in that day, I would not be able to hand crank a car. I had paid an extra $100.00 to have a starter attached to the mechanical device. You pulled a handle on a chain. As you did so you would hear a sound of "B-uzz-rrrR." It kept spitting this sound back at you. After the sixth or seventh time you did this the car would start. I can still recall how the doctor looked so startled when he stopped by to see me "off." He heard the car sputter and asked, "Is this a self-commencer on this thing?"

Following this unusual experience, the Bishop of the Methodist Church and his cabinet of six district superintendents were most gracious. They assigned my wife and me to Gaylord, Michigan, the high spot of land in the Lower Peninsula of Michigan. God pity the people but my wife and I had a wonderful time in Gaylord. We had what people would now call "a ball."

For eight years we had no children. But, it was here in Gaylord that two were born at one time.

Just the Sunday before the twins were born a Mr. Frank Shipp, at that time vice-president of the Bank of Gaylord, left the church door saying to me, "You are a little runt—for a minister." Frank Shipp was the captain of Albion's football team the year they defeated Notre Dame.

A few days later when the twins were born Mr. Shipp was prompted to sit down and write me a letter saying, "I want to apologize for what I said last Sunday about your being a little runt of a man. You are the best man in Gaylord."

Two caterpillars were in the grass when a very beautiful butterfly flew close over them. One said to the other, "I wouldn't get in one of those things for anything in the world." *(Paul Harvey)*

ONE OF HIS SAINTS

Back at the time of World War I, we were serving the Gaylord Church. In those days we had class meetings 30 minutes before the morning worship service. At the early Sunday morning meetings people told of their own religious experience.

Brother Harry Miller was a saintly class leader in his early 90s. His silver gray hair against the cathedral stained glass windows was everything but a halo as he led the class on a Sunday morning.

This very religious man carried a little leather-covered New Testament, about two and one-half inches by three and one-half inches in size. This book, so precious to him, was carried in his shirt pocket over his heart during the Civil War. In one of the more severe battles of this war when men were falling all around him this man came through. A bullet stopped three-quarters of the way through this miniature Word of God, over his heart.

Before Harry Miller died he gave me this Testament. It was one of my most precious possessions. Someone got it away from me. This is one account I expect to settle in eternity!

What doth the Lord require of thee, but to do justly and to love mercy, and to walk humbly with thy God. *(Micah 6:8)*

RECEPTION IN A BAR

Most churches, large or small, think they must have a reception for the new minister and his family. Our beautiful church in a mining town in the Upper Peninsula had a program and reception.

This church had an out appointment by the name of Quinnesec, which in Indian means "Smoky Waters." This small church wanted much to follow along and do the socially correct thing, just as the larger church in town had done. They did not have a basement or reception room of any kind. Their dilemma was "What to do?"

They finally held the reception in an abandoned building. After the program and refreshments my good wife said to me, "What is all that beautiful mahogany and glass up against the wall?" I told friend wife that because it was the prohibition era, many bars were necessarily abandoned. Yes, it was just that! An abandoned bar was where the preacher and his family were treated to the reception. This was a good gesture. It was a new kind of reception for the minister, "Reception In a Bar."

I cannot keep the birds of the air from flying above my head, but I can keep them from building a nest in my hair. *(Martin Luther)*

87

KEY PEOPLE

I had one trip in winter where I had one meal at home out of 33, but the sad part of it all was that I was only touching the fringe of the job.

One of the largest tasks of my ministry is the finding of "Key People" who endeavor to carry on between my visits. One of the greatest satisfactions of this field work is the helping of the people who need guidance into sanitariums, hospitals, etc. Sometimes it demands the renting of a cot, a pail of ice, a hurried trip to a station, the asking for an order to hold a train, a telephone for an improvised ambulance, and sometimes paying for things you order. But we must ask the question, "What would Jesus do?"

In this spirit I want to live and serve, and I ask your guidance when you deem it of any help to me or to the people I serve.

Surely our task is an economic problem as well as a spiritual one. These are days when I would give most anything to have access to a vault that would enable me to minister to some of the needy folk I find. It's not enough to say "God Bless You" to a fellow that's hungry. Then too, if we were rich enough to have a car at Marquette and one on the east end of this never-ending district, if not one on the west as well, we might spend much more time at work and minister to more people with less effort than trying to make a six-year-old Ford do it all. But wishes are not horses. We must do all the best we can with what we have in hand. I pray for guidance to do the right thing as each day becomes a day of many choices. After all this is life, to choose the right and leave undone the wrong.

Sometimes God uses some of His "Key People" to help answer our prayers. Two different groups gave me new Fords and another group a new Chevrolet. God bless them all and more of their kind.

CANOE

Sol Freeman and the "Portable Preacher" would have someone take a canoe in a truck and drive us to Eckerman. Here we would put the canoe in the East Branch of the Tahquamenon River. We would drift along downstream with the current, using a fine wire metal pinch bug to clip onto a bush, so the canoe (so to speak) would ride at anchor.

We would often let out 60 feet of line in the middle of the stream between the high tag alders. By the time we had fished about five miles of the stream in this manner we came in with trout that made the eyes of the natives bulge.

I remember once when a conductor on Number Seven had us showing the catch to all the passengers on the train and he was not satisfied until the men in the baggage car saw the catch, too.

*"Come unto me and I will make
you to be fishers of men."*

For years we had a pass on all the railroads in the Upper Peninsula of Michigan. The Duluth South Shore had a road bed of sand. As each train went by, there was about a quarter of a mile of dust. This reminded me of the drought farther South. It is said the Baptists went to sprinkling, the Methodists used a damp cloth, and the Presbyterians issued rain checks.

COLD TEA

It was the first day of hunting season. We left Newberry long before daylight, and stopped the car about seven miles south of Grand Marais on Superior's southern shore. There was light tracking snow, covered with a thin layer of crisp ice. It definitely was not a hunting day, even if if was the first day of the season. When you walked, the deer could hear the ice crunch a quarter of a mile away. Deer would not move on this brittle ice as it would reveal their whereabouts. (Deer have a lot more patience than mankind.)

We went eastward about three-quarters of a mile into the hardwoods. Nothing moved—not even a squirrel. About 10:00 o'clock, we started to work our way back because we had a funeral that afternoon. Part way out we stopped and sat on a big pine stump to eat our lunch. We had a flat-bottle of cold tea which sat on the stump beside me.

Suddenly, I heard brush breaking and said to myself, "That's it! Stop to eat lunch and the deer will come." Instead, it turned out to be a man, greatly excited. "Well," he said. "My compass has gone wrong." Then he asked, "Which way to the deer run in this upper country?" I asked, "Have you ever hunted before?" "No," he said. "I live in Flint, and I thought you could always depend on your compass." Then he added, "My partners are lost."

This fellow kept watching me eat, now and then taking a sip out of my bottle. Finally, he said, "You got the idea! That's the way to keep warm. It's a wonder you wouldn't offer a fellow a drink!" My bottle sat on the stump beside me. I said, "I'm sorry! Help yourself!"

The hunter hurriedly took about five quick swallows before discovering it was only tea. Then he began to swear and spit, and spit and swear. Finally he said, "That was a terrible trick." Whereupon I replied, "The next time you leave Flint and take a ferry across the Straits into the Upper Peninsula to hunt, believe your compass. Your compass is alright. It's men that get lost, not the compass."

"I'm going out to the highway soon," I said, motioning west.

"Oh," he said, "it's not *that* way."

I came back with, "Are you with the men in the green trailer on the Seney-Grand Marais highway?"

"Yes," he said. "That's my party."

I replied, "Soon as I finish my lunch I am going to my car out by the green trailer. Just follow me, and the next time you come up here and run into a Methodist preacher in the woods, don't ask him for a drink." He raised both hands in the air and said, "Oh, my God!"

After a few rods I asked him to follow my tracks, and led the way. "How do I know anything about tracks?" he said. "They go the wrong way." I said, "Those are my tracks, coming *in*. If we follow them we will come to the green trailer. Now, if you are new in the woods, I'd a lot rather have you in front of me than behind me, with that gun!"

When we reached the trailer, he was shaking. I said, "Brother, after this you believe your compass. You will find moss ofttimes on the north side of the trees, and most of the trees in this region lean to the northeast. And, I must confess, what I know about the woods I learned from the Indians."

The world has a lot of wonderful folks;
Every now and then someone remembers that.

You can't preach on earth and board in heaven.
God bless their kind!

COUNTRY DOCTOR

Smiling "Doc" had a big practice among the poor. He did not have fine clothes, new cars, or half-days off. And he made night calls. Five hundred people attended his funeral.

His bank book showed a balance of $273.00. But in a drawer under his much-used Bible they found another record book on which he had written "My Savings Up There."

This book showed many names. After each he had scrawled a brief note. After one he had written, "Bill's kids need clothes more than I need $50.00." After another, "I couldn't save Sally. I can't charge and I won't let her go to the potter's field." Still another read, "They haven't any money and it's Christmas." After an item of $200.00 he had written, "Paid in full by the smiles and thanks of five little children."

When the doctor's spiritual estate is administered in the court of heaven, people will doubtless be asking each other, "Wouldn't you like to have old Doc's bank account—up there?"

PRAYER: Almighty God, give us the wisdom to recognize the treasure that is eternal. Give us the love and courage to attain it. In Jesus' Name. AMEN

"Lay up for yourselves treasures in heaven."—Matthew 6:20

Mildred Pound

By permission.

4,144 BABIES

When I moved from Gaylord to the Upper Peninsula in 1919, I soon became acquainted with Doctor George Barnett of Ishpeming, Michigan. His background, if I remember correctly, was New York and Wisconsin. He was a graduate of the Rush Medical School of Chicago. Doctor Barnett was one of the outstanding characters on life's way.

When Doctor Barnett came to Ishpeming, he became interested in civic life and for many years was mayor of Ishpeming.

Iron ore mining was the occupation of a great many of the people to whom he ministered as their physician in the Ishpeming area. In Doctor Barnett's day, a physician went into the homes of his patients and ministered to them there. He was a Presbyterian and lived in Ishpeming 47 years. He died December 4, 1935.

Doctor Barnett delivered 4,144 babies. This group included 117 pair of twins. One woman gave birth to 17 babies and Doctor Barnett took care of 14 of them. (I believe her first three children were born in Finland.)

One Finnish woman in Ishpeming said that she must have been the doctor's best customer as she gave birth to five children, one every 9 months and 17 days! It always seemed to me that this must have been some kind of a world's record . . .

Just think of bringing into the world 4,144 babies?

DOLLAR & A QUARTER AN ACRE

When I was assigned to the church in Norway in the Upper Peninsula of Michigan, I inherited an outside appointment four miles westward. This out appointment was called Quinnesec. This was an Indian name associated with the smokey waters on the Menominee River nearby. This little town of Quinnesec was rich in the early settlement lore of the region.

When the railroad was built in 1877 it stopped at a place called Fumee Creek, one-half mile east of Quinnesec. In those days the engineers did not want to build a bridge over the creek. This became the terminal of the railroad north of Chicago.

Nels Larsen, a kindly man who reminded you of Moses, was one of the early pioneers. The Larsens had 10 children who became leaders in the development of this country. This Larsen family is one of a half-dozen families in which I have had the joy of performing four wedding ceremonies.

In this early day of pioneering, roads, railroads and mines were being opened wherever possible. Around Quinnesec a mine was opened in 1875. The Cundy mind was the second mine opened to operation, then came the Vivian and the Indiana mines. The ore from these mines was hauled by oxen and horses and loaded on cars waiting east of Fumee Creek.

A family from Niles, Michigan, bought land five miles west of Quinnesec for only $1.25 an acre or $50.00 a 40. I believe there was something like 112 acres in this tract. They never even saw the land they were negotiating to buy. They bought it from a map. After some years there was a wedding in the family and the old-timers' story is that the preacher was given a deed to 40 acres as a wedding fee. He was not too happy about this 40 so far away.

Years went by and some prospector discovered a high grade of iron ore on this 40 acres of land which had been given as a wedding fee. The minister had long since left Niles but a search was made for him. It took quite some time but he was finally located in a small town on the Pacific coast. He was brought back to Michigan and I am told was given a check for $200,000.00. This was done to clear the title on the 40 acres given as the wedding fee. (Rumor has it that the lawyer who found the preacher man got half the take.)

The people who did the development work on this property started by cutting a road through the timber five miles west from Quinnesec. They started digging a shaft while living in tents but the word of the rich strike brought over 500 souls within a year.

As the mining project continued to grow, a bridge was finally built over Fumee Creek. Once the bridge was constructed, the railroad could be extended another five miles west into the new property and Quinnesec ceased to be the end of the railroad from Chicago. (Today there is a beautiful little park alongside Fumee Creek in the valley just east of Quinnesec. Many tourists, including our family, have had picnic lunches at this precious spot.)

The development of the new mine was begun in 1880. I do not believe that Henry Chapin had anything to do with the workings of the mine, but he was clever enough to secure a contract from the operators that gave him 50 cents a ton royalty on all the ore mined. However, this mine was called the Chapin Mine and became the most productive on the Menominee Range. At the peak of its production, it employed around 2,500 men who in that day worked by candlelight.

This mining property was worked to a depth of 1,520 feet, with a floor of rock and ore left at each 100-foot level. This floor would be shored up with mining timbers called props. At the height of the operation this was the largest underground mine in the world. The mine was closed in 1932; thus the property was worked for over half a century, but during those years they shipped 27,506,869 tons of real high-grade ore. (At 50 cents a ton royalty you can readily see how the Chapins helped to build a very beautiful Presbyterian church in Niles as well as other outstanding landmarks. I believe that in the last years of the operation of this mine, it was owned by a subsidiary of U.S. Steel. This, of course, would not affect the royalty.)

When the timbers began decaying and giving way in the Chapin mine, there was a sinking of many levels of the workings, thus the Milwaukee and St. Paul railroad were left with tracks that were hanging in mid-air. The railroads hauled thousands of tons of rock and fill to build a causeway across a great sunken pit to maintain the level of their tracks. The Michigan State Highway had a matching job trying to keep Highway No. 2 on a level at the top of the 125-150 foot sinking. Today this big pit is in the North Central part of Iron Mountain.

One of the interesting factors in this story is that a descendant of this Chapin family, one Roy D. Chapin, became the head of American Motors.

The Sunday School teacher asked her class how Noah spent his time on the Ark. "Don't you suppose he did a lot of fishing?" she suggested.

"What?" responded one little six-year-old, "with only two worms?" *(Church Bulletin)*

ANGORA SWEATER

Bishop Edgar Blake was one of four Bishops who ever ate in our home. He had been at the beautiful church camp on Lake Michigamme and though it was August it turned desperately cold. We recall how he put newspapers around his body under his coat for protection. The next day he went to the little village of Michigamme and purchased the only sweater he could find for a man of small stature. This sweater was angora in color and while it was not knit for the Episcopacy it, for the time, served a wonderful purpose.

En route to area headquarters, 500 miles from the camp-ground, Bishop Blake and his good wife stopped with us at Newberry for the noonday meal. We lived close to the high school and the children came home to eat. One of our twins, Donn, spoke so often about this beautiful angora sweater (the Bishop had removed his coat). Donn continued speaking about this sweater until we were embarrassed to tears. After dinner the Bishop said, "Donn, you like this sweater, don't you?" then pulled it off and down over the boy's head, saying, "There, I hope this makes a preacher out of you."

Evidently it helped a lot, because it worked!

Let us endeavor so to live that when we die even the undertaker will be sorry.

ALL IN THE DAY'S WORK

It was New Year's Day. We had driven some miles from our regular trail that we might take a father, mother and their four children along with us to church. The folk had gathered at the little country church by the side of the road and we had just made silent prayer and stepped up to announce the first hymn when someone opened the door and called, "Mitt Roat's house is on fire!"

The ring of those words sent a dagger to our hearts. The wind was blowing from 40 to 50 miles an hour and the house was three miles from the church. *(Impossible!)* was the thought that entered our minds . . . but God always expects us to do our best.

The roads were icy and for safety's sake we were just compelled to drive slowly. Our cars gathered up the folk on foot. Soon we had 20 volunteers for a fire department and what a group of fire fighters they were. It is a simple story that cannot be told in a few words. It really was a battle supreme. We battled a terrifically high wind. 'It was not an ox nor an ass or wheat' sifted on the Sabbath Day; but a home (cherished place for all mankind) saved for a man and his family who were much in need of that humble habitation.

This may seem like a peculiar gospel—to leave our hymns unsung and our prayers unsaid to quench a fire that threatened a poor man's all, but we remember the Man of Galilee as He passed through the fields of grain on a Sabbath Day and, as for our unsaid prayers, we cannot forget the mother who said, "I prayed all the way home," and surely God heard that prayer.

A DISASTER AND A FIND

The Barnes-Hecter disaster, probably the worst mining accident in the history of the Lake Superior mining region, located about 28 miles west of Ishpeming on the north side of Highway 28 on the Marquette Range, occurred on the third day of November, 1926, just before noon when the miners would have come to the surface.

The cave-in occurred without any warning and within 15 minutes after the cave-in started the shaft was filled with water to within 150 feet of the surface. In these few minutes the mine contained 450 feet of water.

As I remember, there was a lake or large pond nearby and it seems this may have broken through into the mine. This theory is supported by the fact that a three-foot boulder was carried by the onrushing water and sand part-way down the mine and deposited on a ledge away down the shaft. Superintendents, captains, and engineers were assembled from mines all over the Lake Superior region but no one could account for the accident so the verdict was "Unknown."

Seven bodies were found stripped of clothing by the force of the water and sand and after three days of effort by mining engineers dewatering and reopening the mine was given up rather than risk the loss of additional lives; so the mine itself became the burial ground of most of the men.

Rutherford Wills was working on the second level near the shaft when he heard the onrushing water, called to his partners and fled! He made a dash in the shaft 100 feet up the ladders. Five other men had been to the surface to eat lunch and were descending when they scampered ahead of Wills, back to the surface. Wills was the only *one* working in the mine who escaped, so to this day the Barnes-Hecter

Mine remains a tomb to all but one of the men below ground working on that day shift.

Fifty-one men lost their lives that day in the Barnes-Hecter mine near North Lake. The dead, 40 of them married, included 34 from Ishpeming, 7 from North Lake, 6 from the immediate location of the mine and others scattered around the area.

It was 11:20 a.m. when the cave-in occurred at a point above the first level and in 15 minutes the workings of the mine were filled with sand and water. The muck suggesting that the bottom of a rain-deepened swamp had given way into the diggings rose to within 185 feet of the surface. There was no warning. The men were looking forward to the noon break, when they would come to the surface.

As wives and children huddled at the mine shaft that night, seven bodies were found stripped of clothing by the force of the water. They were found a mile from the Barnes-Hecter shaft, in a tunnel connecting the workings with the Morris Mine. They had run for their lives only to be caught by the onrushing water.

Very close and across the highway from the caved-in Barnes-Hecter Mine was a green schoolhouse known, I believe, as the Barnes School. Ofttimes we would take our lunch in a basket and stop for the evening meal eaten from a spread on the grass by this green schoolhouse. This was quite true if we were working 100 or 150 miles west of Marquette. Instead of riding on a railroad pass, we would in this manner keep the family together.

This particular evening, mother was driving the car; but, after the meal was spread on the grass by the green schoolhouse and we were ready to eat, mother had no appetite.

She discovered that she had lost the diamond from her engagement ring. Donn, our son, must have been 10 years old, but small for his age. He said, "Don't cry, Mama. You know when you pulled the brake lever your diamond probably went right down through that hole in the floor." (The Model "T" cars had a slot about one inch times four and one-half inches through which you worked the hand brake.)

"Oh, child," said Mother, "that is hopeless." But Donn crawled under the car from the eastern side with the western sun shining brightly on the grass and came out saying, "Here's your diamond, Mother!!"

With the precious stone in her purse, she dried her tears and ate with the rest of us.

"Ask and it shall be given you; seek, and ye shall find; knock and it shall be opened unto you."

When I was a young preacher, I was assigned to a new church. This church was heated by a stove with a long stretch of stovepipe overhead. The first Sabbath was a cool day, so someone started a fire. This warmed up a multitude of hornets who enjoyed the heat. While I was making the morning prayer, one of these hornets stung me on the back of the neck. I just reached up my hand and swiped him off. After church a brother said to me, "How on earth did you keep on praying after that hornet stung you?"

I replied, "Just where were your eyes during prayer?"

HOLY MOMENT

Charlie Goff, one of America's great preachers and also an instructor at Garrett Theological Seminary, was also pastor of Chicago Temple. (The big one with the cross atop downtown.)

At a session of the Michigan Annual Conference held in Goodrich Chapel at Albion College, my preacher boy, Donn, happened to be chairman of the evening session. Charlie Goff was to be the featured speaker. After Donn introduced him to the congregation of 1400 ministers and laymen, Dr. Goff walked out to the edge of the platform, pointed back with his left thumb over his shoulder, saying, "My pupil, my pupil, introducing me."

At the close of a most inspiring address he told how his mother came from Iowa to see his new Temple in downtown Chicago's loop. Dr. Goff told how she put her hands behind her, entered that great sanctuary, and walked slowly up that long aisle softly singing, "I can hear my Saviour calling, Take thy cross and follow, follow Me." Dr. Goff was unable to keep back the tears as he witnessed his mother's radiance and reverent joy.

At the close of the challenging address he started slowly down that middle aisle singing as his mother had sung years before, "I Can Hear My Saviour Calling," and immediately that crowd of 1400 surged forward in a new act of re-dedication. It was one holy moment I shall never forget.

THE BIG BOTTLE

The many years that we served as Methodism's Sky Pilot of the Upper Peninsula of Michigan, working in the out-of-way places of the 15 counties north of the Straits of Mackinac, we often took the ferry across the Straits of Mackinac from St. Ignace to Mackinaw City.

Every three months, or four times a year, we would go to Detroit to speak in a different church every day and on three radio stations daily. On the summer trip the children would go with us as far as Bay City, where their grandmother lived. About the time we got off the boat the children would begin, "How long, Daddy? How long before we get to the Big Bottle?"

The Big Bottle was an electric sign in Saginaw which had been erected over Vernor's Emporium. Vernor's ginger ale was an unusual drink at that time, not being sold in the Upper Peninsula. We would hear this question at least two dozen times between Mackinaw and Saginaw. We always stopped to please the children.

At least this was part of the reason, the rest was to make an installment payment on a big debt . . . It was Grandma Vernor who paid for all my books to study for the ministry.

(By the way, we are still working on the payment of that debt.)

Governments are like clocks, run by the works men put in them. *(William Penn)*

HOLY WATER

The Reverend Weldon Crossland, a very popular young minister of Central Church, Pontiac, Michigan, and later at Rochester, New York, toured the Holy Land and brought back a bottle of water from the River Jordan. This he divided with us so that it christened many children with water from the river of Palestine, running down from the north into the Sea of Galilee.

Our youngest was born in a mining town in the Upper Peninsula of Michigan called "Norway." We knew that our superintendent, George Olmstead, was en route by train from Marquette to Hermansville and that he would pass through Norway at 2:40. We asked the conductor to hold the train until we could get this superintendent off the Southbound. We took him to the hospital where he baptized our latest (Doreen), (Mrs. Stanley Johnson, Poway, California) then whirled him in our trembling Ford to his evening session at Hermansville. I will never forget that "Uncle George," as we all called him, said after the ceremony, "This is the *first* time I ever baptized with Holy Water!"

Over a half-century later when Bishop Loder was dedicating the Empire Church, he said, as we burned the mortgages, "I want all of you folks to know that this is *Holy* Smoke!!"

Eve: Do you really love me?
Adam: Who else?
(Maturity Magazine)

SPIRITS IN A BAGGAGE CAR

One day we were riding train No. One on the *Duluth South Shore* and *Atlantic* between Trout Lake (A-17) and Marquette, Michigan (155) (Station numbers that you filled in on your pass slip) when a conductor whom I had learned to know well came to us and said, "I can't keep my men in the baggage car. There is a corpse up there and they are really afraid. I wish you would come up to the smoker and we will take those fellows who are afraid to ride up there because they say the corpse gurgles. Come with me and see if you can calm them down."

I said to the baggage men, "Dead men don't talk and dead men don't gurgle when the undertaker finishes with them." Nevertheless, they did not want to stay in that baggage car. I said, "Here, fellows, get hold of the handles on this rough box, let's move this thing three or four feet and see what happens. See if he still gurgles?"

We moved the rough box about four feet and a broken steam pipe in the floor of the baggage car started to imitate "Old Faithful" out in the Yellowstone National Park!

In Denver, a Sunday School class was asked to set down their favorite Biblical truths. One youngster printed, "Do to others as others do one to you." *(Less Olson - Denver Post)*

TALES OF THE SEA

Long, long ago my father grew up as a boy in the state of Maine. The day came when things were not going too well—as happens in the lives of most, if not all, boys sooner or later. My grandfather was indignant and threatened to give my father a "licking," as it was then called. My father, although he was only a boy of 12 at the time, did not intend to take a thrashing for something he did not do. The misunderstanding had reached a climax. Threatened by his father and hurt because his father could not believe that he actually did not do this, my father countered his dad with this remark:

"Dad, if you lick me for that when I did not do it, I'll leave home." Well, he got a good spanking, nevertheless; and, he kept his word.

He left.

Because they had lived so near the coast the only logical place that he could run to was the sea.

After spending time as a novice on a vessel and learning the "ropes" of life at sea, he decided he was ready to sign in on a new ship. He signed up. When it came time for them to change crews, here was his brother on the same ship.

On that voyage, they ran into a terrific storm. The older brother went aloft to fix some rigging. He was blown off into the sea and drowned. The crew retrieved him, but he had inhaled so much salt water that his was a hopeless case. He could not survive.

For years my parents displayed in our home a picture of father's brother with his sweetheart. (He had been buried at sea, finally.) The picture which he'd had in his clothes, at the time of the accident, was heavily spotted with great blobs of brine. Whenever you looked at the picture you had a strange feeling of being "squeezed" or choked within yourself.

My father spent many years of his early life at sea. He touched all of the continents except Australia. He experienced many expeditions on whaling vessels. This, he always told us, had been a rough phase of his life.

Once when they were on a merchant vessel, they lost their cargo of wheat and were shipwrecked in Hamburg, Germany. To be stranded in Germany, in those days, meant you would do five years of military service in the army. The two young men, my father and his chum, had to find a way out of this possibility. When an English ship came in, they immediately went to the captain with this dilemma. When they asked if they could go on his boat the captain said:

"You boys know only too well that I would lose my papers if I were to take you aboard this ship. Now, get the hell out of here, but remember that this boat leaves here at 12 o'clock tonight."

After the boat was a few miles out of port, the boys who were stowed away on top of some coal heard him say to the First Mate, "You have two boys as stowaways on board. Hunt them up and put them to work." The boys overheard this and came crawling out from the heap of coal. He said to the big fellow, "Can you cut hair?"

The boy answered, "I never cut hair in my life."

"All right," said the Mate. "Go down below and shovel that coal." Then he turned to my father and asked him the same question, "Kid, can you cut hair?"

"Sure," said dad. (He did not want to shovel that coal.) Thus, he became the ship's barber for 18 months.

Once, on another English boat, they pulled into the port of Genoa, Italy, with a cargo of coal. The ship's crew wanted to unload the coal with some sort of windlass machinery (but the Italians who were the dock workers wanted to carry it off in buckets and make the job last.) The result was a "free for all." The Italians blew out all of the lights. In the darkness the English cook said, "All of you lie flat on the floor."

Then this cook took a meat cleaver and went after the Italians who had not been told to lie down and were on their feet. Two or three men were killed and a number of others were injured.

Before the fight was over my father, who was not even directly involved in it at all, had been stabbed in the chest. This was a long deep gash and he was in the hospital in Genoa, Italy, for six weeks. He carried this scar to his grave.

Another time father was on a ship loaded with wheat. The vessel had sailed out of the mouth of the Mississippi River. It was bound for Hamburg, Germany. They ran into a severe typhoon and were tossed around in the Gulf of Mexico for three days. After this, they were blown back into the mouth of the Mississippi River. Some idea of the rampaging waves can be gained when we recall that they had a bear chained on deck and this huge bear was just washed overboard.

In those days it was difficult to find men who were experienced enough and would spend their time on a whaling vessel. When it was time for boats to go out on a "whaling job," as they called it, more than one method was used to conscript or "Shanghai" the crew.

Once and only once my father had the unfortunate experience of accepting a job which he never really agreed to perform in the first place. Men were hired to act as a "shanghaier." Today, we might call him perhaps not a "hit" man, but at least a hustler.

A professional "shanghaier" managed to somehow get my father "drunk." In a deep stupor he and others were loaded aboard a big boat. When father awakened he found that the boat was well at sea. Somehow, his name was on the ship's register. The whaling boat was at sea for months. All the men aboard led a terrible life. It was a rough occupation. The food was mostly whale meat. The storms were numerous. The monotony was deadly. The work was dangerous. It was all the more difficult because most of the men had not been given a chance to choose this life.

Like my father, they too, had been shanghaied.

Once the boat had to put in at the Cape Verde Islands, a group of Portuguese islands on the equator, off the coast of Africa. Something had to be done to keep the sailors from deserting the ship. (When men did desert a ship, if they were recaptured they had to serve out the rest of their term without pay.) In spite of this, the time at sea had been so long and unbearable that six of the men decided to leave the ship—in spite of the fact that the ship had been anchored a mile offshore for this express purpose of curtailing any deserters.

Of the six men who decided to leave, one of them was a non-swimmer. The other men took the grindstone out of the frame. With the non-swimmer on the wooden frame they swam and towed him ashore. Four of the deserters, including the non-swimmer, were caught. Father and a buddy hid out in a fruit cellar. The Portuguese people knew what had happened and supplied them with food. (Father and his friend had some money sewed in their underclothes.) After six long weeks the whaling ship set sail. Then, father and his partner came out of the cellar and stayed around the docks.

They were offered a job breaking stones for 12 cents a day for a breakwater. Somehow, they were not very interested in this—just as long as their money held out. They lived well and quite inexpensively, mostly on fresh fruits. It didn't matter too much to them for they were away from the whale meat, away from the dull days they had known—days of just playing cards, working, fighting and dreading to get up in the morning. This was behind them. Something better would happen—in time. And, it did.

In a few weeks an English vessel came into port. These two young but experienced seamen offered their assistance as crew members, with pay. They were quickly accepted and soon they were on board ship again and this time they were bound for England.

Money is good but make sure you haven't lost the things it cannot buy. *(Unknown)*

* * *

I believe it was Henry Ford who said, "Luck is pluck with the *P* worked off."

* * *

Every temptation is great or small according as the man is. *(Jeremy Taylor)*

* * *

She's the picture of the father and the sound track of her mother. *(Earl Wilson)*

* * *

When you flee temptation be sure you don't leave a forwarding address. *(Irish Digest)*

* * *

Wisdom is knowing when to speak your mind and when to mind your speech. *(Ralph W. Emerson)*

* * *

The ships that come in while we sit and wait are mostly hardships. *(Henry Fredrick)*

* * *

There's one good thing about snoring; it's so simple you can do it in your sleep. *(Central Church Bulletin)*

5' 16"

The oldest members of the Detroit Conference remember with pride and awe, Seth Reed, the grand old man of Michigan Methodism, a circuit rider in Michigan's wilderness who also founded some of our most important modern institutions. Seth Reed's career will never be duplicated.

As a boy he suffered greatly from asthma. He was given the unhappy nickname of "Death on Stilts." Who would have guessed that he was destined to live over a century?

Early in life he taught a neighborhood school for $5.00 a month and boarded around, but he was always looking for opportunities to learn. He attended an academy in Erie County, New York. His staple articles of food were bread, rolls and potatoes roasted in the coals of a fireplace. Academically he stood near the top. He taught one school in which he had 13 different kinds of reading books. Among other subjects he taught surveying, a subject very important on the frontier.

Seth Reed sensed the religious hunger of the frontier. He was often asked to read a sermon or give an exhortation. At the suggestion of many friends his mind turned toward the ministry; so at the close of his last school he was prepared to say to this friends and to the church, "If I am wanted as a herald of salvation to lost men, Here am I; send me."

On the closing day of school a young girl wrote these lines to some closing verse:

> "Go then, dear friend, your Master calls,
> Go sound the trump from Zion's walls.
> The work is great, the work is good,
> To call lost sinners home to God."

Little did Seth Reed dream that later he would marry this very young girl.

In 1844 the Conference set Grand Rapids apart as a station. The rest of the circuit which comprised all of Montcalm County, part of Ionia County as well as part of Ottawa County, was assigned to David Whitlock and Seth Reed. Whitlock preached but twice, was stricken with pneumonia and died, leaving this tremendous circuit to young Seth Reed. He went around once in four weeks preaching 20 to 24 times. He did well with his conference studies doing most of his studies while riding horseback.

The salary of a Methodist preacher was then fixed at $100.00 a year for a single man and $200.00 a year for a married man with $16.00 added for each child. Reverend Reed told a story how one year he received a salary including hay, oats, socks, mittens and cash of $59.56.

Seth Reed was sent to hold a camp meeting in the Saginaw Valley, somewhere on the Cass River. His last sermon to the Indians was on the text, "They that wait upon the Lord shall mount up with wings as Eagles." When he had finished the sermon, the leader came up and gave him the Indian name meaning "Straight Up Through the Sky." He told how they found themselves in a nest of yellow jackets, whom he said, "Seemed delighted in impressing their inverted blessings upon us!"

In pioneer days the road from Flint to Saginaw lay through much swamp and then there was much corduroy road (logs laid side by side with no earth thereon). One stretch of this road leading into Saginaw had six miles of this corduroy road. At the close of the conference the Bishop was reading the appointments. In those days no preacher was supposed to know where he was going until his name was read. The Bishop was reading the list when the presiding elder whispered to Reed, "You are going to Saginaw." Seth Reed replied, "I can't move my wife over that six miles of corduroy." Whereupon the presiding elder slipped up to the Bishop and whispered something in his ear; so it was that he took his pen and scratched out "Saginaw" and it then read: "Saginaw Mission, Andrew

Bell; Genesee Circuit, Seth Reed." Seth Reed said, "I do not know whether my eldest daughter knew how she helped the Bishop make the appointments that fall."

In 1853-1855, Seth Reed served at Monroe. In the Monroe Sunday School was a very mischievous lad called George Custer, later well-known as an army general. This became the man who lost out with the Indians at Custer's Last Stand, where he died from an overdose of arrows. After Monroe, Reverend Reed was sent to Ann Arbor. He felt embarrassed to go as a relatively uneducated man to a college town but he went—resolved to do his best. After Ann Arbor he served Port Huron, which gave him a large watch which he was still carrying 45 years later.

Reed was preaching in a schoolhouse on one occasion where there was a bench across the rear of the room where a bunch of rowdies were very distracting. Reed said that at another point on his circuit he had one boy who acted the same way but he said nothing. At the close someone said, "We are glad that you did not reprimand the boy because he is an idiot." Reed had no more trouble with the folks on the bench.

In 1859, Seth Reed was sent to Woodward Avenue Church in Detroit. The official board at its first meeting raised his salary $200.00 a year, making it $1000.00, the highest salary in Michigan Methodism. He later preached at Ypsilanti, then served some time with the army in Civil War days. Here he would aid the surgeons, give food and drink and point the dying with prayers to Jesus, and often give Christian burial.

After the Civil War he served as financial agent for Albion College and helped to raise a large amount of money. He was one of the committee chosen to select the site which turned out to be Bay View, north of Petoskey. He was secretary of Bay View for 13 years and it was on his motion that the place was given the name of Bay View.

The title of presiding elder was changed to district superintendent. (To me the title presiding elder always sounded churchy, but the term district superintendent sounded like the supervisor of a chain of hardware stores.)

113

But this was still a great task to guide a number of preacher men and help the Bishop make appointments. In this capacity Seth Reed served the church 18 of the years of his ministry. I believe it was George Elliot who wrote of him:

"He was not old in soul or body. Both ears and eyes worked well. He used no glasses for reading or anything else. *He never accepted discharge from the army of God.* No one more gloriously attained the beauty of age—and Indian summer as lovely as Spring, a sunset as glorious as the dawn."

At the Conference of 1913, at age 90, he was asked to speak to the conference. He spoke for an hour and a half on "The Story of My Life." For 79 successive years he answered the roll call at conference.

When I was serving the Gaylord church during World War I, this man preached for me when he was 96 years old. If he paused, his wife would say one word, like "Bear," and he was off telling us about the time when he was walking alone on Grand River Road when he saw a bear and her cub coming toward him through the bushes. The bear did not see him until within a few feet of him. The bear stood up on her hind legs and opened her mouth wide. He stood on all his legs and opened his eyes wide. He was studying natural history. She was studying theology, I suppose. He went on to tell how the cub climbed a tree. In a few minutes a man came along with a cane which turned out to be a gun, and he shot the cub. He finished by saying, "I escaped with a thankful heart and a good story to tell."

Reverend Reed studied as he rode in the saddle. One day a tree had fallen across the trail and lodged in another tree. He did not see the tree until his head hit it and the tree scraped him right off the horse, saddle and all. The horse went on about four miles where they often stopped at a log house. The man said to his wife, "Let us kill a chicken. Brother Reed will be along pretty soon—if he is alive."

The Saturday night before he preached for me I told my good wife to be sure and cook oatmeal for breakfast, because of Brother Reed's age. His wife and I both ordered cornflakes. After Brother Reed had been served his oatmeal he said, "Sister Doten, what have I done that I can't have cornflakes like other folks?" With reddened face I said, "Well, I guess it's time for me to go to confession. I told my good wife to give you oatmeal." After mother had exchanged his oatmeal for flakes he turned on me and said, "And now, young fellow, I'd have you know I'm eating these flakes with the teeth God gave me." I shall never forget *one* thing he said in his sermon that day. He said, "I preached in Lansing when there were four log houses there."

Seth Reed was six feet, four inches tall, but if you were to ask how tall he was he would always reply, "Five-foot-sixteen." He had a flowing white beard that came to his waistline. As young men entered the conference they would ask, "Who is the tall man with the long white beard?" Then we would reply, "Why, don't you know? That's Moses!"

This same man preached in our church in Sault Ste. Marie, Michigan, on the Sunday nearest his 100th birthday. Not long after I watched him walk to the altar and saw the Bishop give him 100 long-stemmed red roses.

For many years Seth Reed held the Methodist Conference Cane. This is a very plain, gold-headed cane. Seth Reed held it longer than any man. Today in the Michigan Conference I believe there is one man older than the writer. Anyhow, I am not too sure that I want this trophy. (Someone might just be lurking to swipe it for the top.)

After a fall on March the 24th, 1924, Seth Reed passed from time into eternity, at the age of 100 years, 9 months and 22 days. The funeral was conducted by the beloved Bishop Theodore Henderson in the Court Street Church in Flint, Michigan. It was the earthly echo of the coronation of a saint which had already taken place in a world of endless glory.

REVEREND SETH REED

"WHAT'S THE STRING?"

Over a half century ago I was assigned with a group of two dozen men on a college campaign for Dickinson College in Pennsylvania and Pennington School for boys in New Jersey. I drew one very interesting card but, with 50 some years gone by, for the life of me I cannot recall his name, so we will just re-name the chap "John Watson."

In spite of the loss of his name, I can still see this 225-pounder as if it were yesterday. He was a real estate dealer in a suburb of Philadelphia. I remember going on a Reading suburban railroad one cold November morning.

When I entered this real estate office at 9:30 this big fellow rose and came to me and said, "I have a deal on here. If you will just be seated on the davenport in the big window, I will see you later."

This was a black leather davenport and cold as it could be on a bleak November day. I read and shivered, then shivered and read, until 20 minutes to 12. This big fellow closed the deal and ushered his clients out. It was then he turned to me and said, "Well, I just made $7500.00 on that deal. Now, I will take you out to lunch and we will see what you want."

We were partway through lunch when the big chap said, "Well, what's on your mind?" I replied by saying, "If I were to say Dickinson College would it ring a bell?" "Oh," he said, "you are on that college drive."

I said, "You know, if I had a brother who attended Dickinson College who was loved up and down the land as he was, who just a few weeks ago went into God's great tomorrow and I made $7500.00 in a forenoon, I would give it to Dickinson College as a memorial to my brother." He looked me straight in the eye for a full minute, then he said, "Under one condition." I said, "What's the string?" He came back with, "That you come back Sunday morning and get matching money from the congregation." Then he added, "I'm the Lay Leader and I will fix it with the minister." I replied, "It's a deal, only get me the last ten minutes."

Sunday morning found a crowded church. The preacher found a stopping place in exactly 17 minutes. It was then I challenged the people for the matching money. I remember we came through with far more than another $7500.00. Ofttimes it takes real courage to do what needs doing for the King of Kings.

"Ask and ye shall receive."

NEW YEAR'S RECIPE

Take two heaping cups of patience,
One heartful of love,
Two handfuls of generosity,
A dash of laughter,
One handful of understanding,
Sprinkle generously with kindness,
Add plenty of faith,
Spread over a period of a lifetime,
And serve to everybody you meet.
(Unknown)

ODD WEDDING FEES

When I was a young preacher, we had an outstanding minister in our church on the west side of Bay City, Michigan, by the name of John Gregory.

In this congregation was the Handy family. Tom Handy operated coal mines in and about that region, and built a railroad east out through the thumb of Michigan. The Handys had a wedding in their family and paid the preacher with a bag of beans.

When I was young, flour generally came in cloth sacks. Women would wash these sacks, put them out in the sun to bleach out the printing on them, then use them for dish towels, sometimes linings for homemade caskets and many useful things. When I was a boy I recited many poems and one of them was the one about paying the preacher with a bag of beans.

The Handys took this poem literally and filled a 25-pound sack with beans as the wedding fee . . .

After about six weeks Mrs. Gregory, the minister's wife, dipped into the sack and took out a dipper of beans to look over, wash and bake. When she dumped them out on a newspaper, she found a $20 gold piece. Her husband, the Reverend John Gregory, said, "I'll get the wash tub," and in this tub they found *four* more $20 gold pieces, so there was $100 of gold in that bag of beans. This was back in the day when the preacher received $5 for marrying a couple.

Sometime ago, there was a softball player and a baseball pitcher who changed their previous plans for a church wedding and were married in their ball field attire, in the dugout, behind the baseball diamond.

Another couple met in the lunchroom at Trout Lake, which was the crossing of two leading railroad systems of the Upper Peninsula, the *Duluth South Shore* and *At-*

lantic and the *Soo* Line. The bridegroom was an engineer on the *Soo* system and the bride a waitress in the lunch-room. This couple gave up their well-laid plans for a wedding, and were married in the outfits they wore on the day they met: the groom in his blue-jean engineer outfit with the customary red handkerchief around the neck, and she in her gingham dress. He ran a passenger train, and she the home, and they were quite some couple.

One morning, about daylight, I stepped off the train in Hulbert, Michigan, between the Soo Junction and Sault Ste. Marie, Michigan. A young Norwegian greeted me and said, "I want to g-g-get m-m-married today." I replied, "Laddie, you have to have a girl for that," and he shot back, "Oh, I got her, all right." He told me his girl lived in a little shack northeast of the village. I told him that I would see him at the post office at 11 o'clock. (I wanted some time to learn something about these youngsters.) All my inquiries led to one answer, "He would never have much, but he would be good to her." About two o'clock that afternoon on a dull April day, I married them. He in a heavy gray woolen suit (evidently from the Soo Woolen Mills), and she in her homemade dress.

When the ceremony was over, he said, "Preacher, how much do I owe you now?" I said, "Oh, you can give me what you think she is worth." His brother spoke up and said, "Frank, do you think she is worth 35 cents?" He said, "I'll tell you what I'm going to do. I am going to give you a brand new bill," and he came across the room and gave me a brand new one dollar bill.

When the night express took me home, I walked up the hill to the place called "Home," and gave my wife this new dollar bill. She said, "You rascal, I think you kept nine of this!"

One night about midnight when it was pouring down rain, a couple awakened me to be married. I borrowed on my patience a bit, as I looked at their boots heavy with dark blue clay. They seemed to keep hurrying me more and more until I could resist no longer. Then I said, "If you people were in such a hurry to get this done, why on earth did you not come today?'' Her only answer for this was that her mother had been married so many years ago today and she wanted to be married on the same date.

When the papers were properly signed and they were hurrying to leave, the young boy said, ''Preacher, we forgot to tell you, we do not have any money.''

''Well, now you have a wife,'' I said. ''Be good to her.'' With this they went out into the darkness of a stormy night, and the preacher folk, to bed.

Eight long years later, we received a letter from Northwestern Canada. To my good wife, Iva, I said, ''Who on earth do we know up there?'' We opened the letter and in a woman's handwriting we read together, ''Eight years ago we awakened you one night during a storm to marry us. That night my husband lied to you. He told you we had no money.

''For two years now we have been going to church and trying to do what is right.

''Enclosed you will find a money order for $20. Ten is for marrying us and ten is for waiting eight years for your money.'' Conscience had done its work and conscience had done it well.

A small boy in a department store was standing near the escalator watching the moving handrail. ''Something wrong?'' asked the clerk.

''Nope,'' said the lad, ''just waiting for my gum to come back.'' *(Central Church Bulletin)*

MORTAL IMMORTALS

At the opening of an annual conference the secretary calls the roll of the ministers who died during the year, after which someone gives a memorial address.

Merton S. Rice, Methodism's great preacher of his generation, was for 30 years the minister of Metropolitan Methodist Church of Detroit. Year after year Dr. Rice had been asked before to give this memorial address. Always, he promised but somehow found a way of retreat by giving a lecture or taking some other engagement so that someone else had to substitute.

In 1931 the writer happened to be chairman of this memorial committee. At the conference session the year before I had asked Dr. Rice to give this address and as usual, he accepted. Knowing the number of times he had worked his way out of it, I wrote him as follows: "Dr. Rice, It has come to my attention that year after year you have slipped out of the conference memorial. This time, the tacks that hold this number to this year's program have been dipped in concrete, there is no retreat."

Following is the answer in his own handwriting. And he did a masterful job with "Mortal Immortals."

I'd rather sit on a pumpkin and have it all to myself than to be crowned on a velvet cushion. *(Victor Hugo)*

M. S. RICE
C. B. ALLEN
PASTORS

METROPOLITAN
METHODIST EPISCOPAL CHURCH
WOODWARD AND CHANDLER AVES.
DETROIT, MICH.

7/9/31.

My Dear Doctor Daten —

Bless you for inquiring
re Conference Sermon. Put
it down something thus —
Mortal Immortals. —
and I will see what I can
make out of that —
Blessings on everybody —
Yours, M. S. Rice.

MIRACLE AT THE SOO

St. Augustine, Florida, was founded in 1565; Plymouth Colony in 1620, and Sault Ste. Marie, the oldest settlement in Michigan and the third oldest in the United States was founded as a fur trading post in the early 1600s. In 1668, Fr. Marquette founded the first Mission and named it La Sault de St. Marie. The Sault means "Long Falls," or terror-striking mile, of white water rapids of the St. Mary's River rushing from Lake Superior down into Lake Huron.

The Indians portaged their canoes around this treacherous mile. As development opened, cargoes were unloaded both above and below the rapids and drawn around the tumbling waters by oxen and horses. Finally a narrow gauge railroad was built along what today is Portage Avenue and cargoes were moved by oxen, mule or horse on these flimsy rails, thus skirting the wild rapids.

What is known as the Toledo War broke out in 1835. This was a war between Ohio and Michigan Territory. Both parties made ready to fight over the strip of land that contained Toledo. In fact, 200 Michiganders invaded Toledo, pulled down their flag and dragged it through the streets. President Andrew Jackson stepped in and effected a compromise whereby Ohio retained the strip of land but the Michigan Territory was given the Upper Peninsula as a peace offering. It was then that Henry Clay said in Congress, "The Upper Peninsula is beyond the remotest regions of the moon." Two years later, in 1837, Michigan was admitted as a state. The name comes from the Indian *Mitchi Sawgyegan* which actually means "Lake Country."

Congress passed an act that granted to the State of Michigan a donation of public lands in exchange for the building of a canal around the Soo Rapids. I believe the State in turn offered something like three-quarter million acres of land for the building of a canal. It was no minor dream. It would be a pathway for commerce if it could be done. There was timber, copper and iron in abundance above those treacherous rapids and something should be done to get around the portaging of cargoes around the Soo Rapids of St. Mary's River.

A salesman by the name of Charles Harvey, who had no time for 'firewater' or even tobacco, found financial backing in the East, especially through the Fairbanks Scales folk, and he tackled the job. One of his handicaps was the loss of 1,600 men by a cholera epidemic while building the canal.

The first canal at the Soo was blasted out to a depth of 12 feet and opened to traffic in the summer of 1855. It comprised two locks 350 feet in length and 70 feet in width. This was but the beginning of a great waterway which overcame a tremendous barrier to commerce.

The early ships paid four cents per ton for the privilege of locking through the canal. In 1877, this was reduced to three cents a ton. In 1881, the Locks were transferred to the United States government and placed under the jurisdiction of the U. S. Army Corps of Engineers and since that time the Locks have been operated toll free.

There are four locks in the Soo system. The Davis Lock built in 1914, the Sabin Lock in 1919, the MacArthur Lock in 1943 and the Poe Lock in 1968. The Poe Lock is the largest lock in the St. Lawrence Seaway and cost $40,000,000.00 to build. It is also the only lock that can carry the large vessels of 105 feet in width. This lock also has the greatest depth, that of 32 feet. The Soo Locks handle the greatest tonnage of any lock system on earth. I am sure if the boats could talk, they would say, "We were on the Big Elevator."

Today the Soo Locks have an international ring. In 1953, 126,000,000 tons of freight passed through the Soo Locks. This seems to have been an all-time high. The average today is somewhere around 100,000,000 tons annually. Many years the tonnage has exceeded that of both the Panama Canal and the Suez Canals combined. This would not be true today with the oil from the Arctic going through the Panama.

Lake Superior lies 21 feet higher than the level of Lake Huron and Lake Michigan. There are 16 gates to control the level of the water in the locks. It takes an average of 30 minutes to enter, then raise or lower the water. About an hour from the time a vessel enters the canal leading to the locks it enters St. Mary's River or Lake Superior.

Further out in the river beyond the locks is the U. S. Hydroelectric Power Plant which generates 150,000,000 kilowatt hours of electric power each year. The surplus power beyond that used for the operation of the locks is sold to private power companies for distribution in factories, homes and other cities.

I was always intrigued by the special timber lookers who covered the hardwood forests of the Upper Peninsula looking for bird's-eye maple trees. They could spot the bark that told them the lumber from that tree would be full of curls and small-pox spots, very beautiful. They might find but three or four trees in a tract of timber, but they would fell these trees and get the logs out to a spur siding of the railroad. After they had a few logs at a number of spurs, they would load a few logs at the western end of the Peninsula, have an engine move the car east to another spur, load a few more logs and by the time it reached the mills at the Soo the car would be loaded to capacity. Here the mill cut the slabs off the outside making large square timbers and these were shipped to France for the making of bird's-eye maple furniture. So the traffic not only bore limestone and coal, but timber, copper and iron as well as grain from the northwest.

When we lived in Newberry, we often took a picnic basket and went to the Soo 67 miles away to buy woolens. We would eat our basket lunch on the grass by the Soo Locks. It was such a thrill for the children to see the big ships come up the St. Mary's River, enter the locks and be lifted 21 feet by water, then steam out into the "Big Shining Sea Water" (Gitchi Gummee). If you want a bird's-eye view of the greatest waterway in the world, just cross over into Canada on the International Bridge.

YOU CAN'T DO THAT AT OUR HOUSE

Once in awhile, we would spend an afternoon and an evening in a woodchopper's camp. We had been in this camp about six months before, and they knew the portable preacher was coming this Thursday night. It was the best tar paper shack in the woodchopper's village.

The mother had a treat for the family (the preacher was coming). She made gingerbread. At supper time I had a little lard left on my plate. This we were using for butter. I turned up my gingerbread and used up the bit of lard I had on the bottom of my cake. A little boy lay down his tools and looked me straight in the eye and said, "Butter on cake, hey? You can't do that at our house."

DAYS AND NIGHTS
IN UPPER MICHIGAN

Travelling on railroads, snowshoes, horse drawn drays, the ends of orange boxes when without snowshoes, preaching in dance halls, sleeping on tables: the Methodist Home Missionary carries on.

—Editor, World Service News '29

The Upper Peninsula of Michigan, which is known to Methodism as the Marquette District, is almost 400 miles east and west and 200 miles from tip to tip north and south, has over 1600 miles of shoreline on the Great Lakes and almost 11,000,000 acres of farming, mining and timberlands. One soon learns that the eastern end is north of Detroit and the western end lacks four miles of being straight north of Davenport, Iowa.

The work of the past winter was, at times, almost an endurance test, especially so because of the fact that the North country witnessed the hardest winter in 20 years. Out of a circuit demanding almost a sermon a day, we missed only four services in a year. I have travelled almost every conceivable way, including railroads, snowplows, horse and dray and, when snowshoes were not available, used the ends of orange crates for substitute snowshoes. It has been my lot to ring the bell, build the fire, cut the wood on the plains and take it with me in the Ford so the smoke from the once famous pines might give evidence of my arrival as well as vie with Jack Frost when we worshiped. But I must not forget to say that the spirit of appreciation shown far exceeds any remuneration I have ever known in my ministry.

Our first funeral on the job called me 115 miles. I once preached all winter in an old dance hall. The township board finally provided a little town hall, making a real cozy chapel for our worship services. I was the undertaker, sexton and preacher. I officiated at a funeral in an Indian home at 8:00 a.m., rode a freight train for six miles and held another funeral at 9:30, then travelled 250 miles to be on time for the Sabbath, arriving at four a.m. Sunday morning. (I slept on a table, because there was less draft than on the floor.) At one time I travelled 735 miles for five services.

We once traveled to Grand Marais during a heavy snow blockade. Grand Marais is located 26 miles from the railroad. On the trail there is an unfinished halfway house in which we would stop and build a fire and eat our sandwich. The trip was undertaken to decide whether or not the inhabitants of this particular town were in need of medical aid. The mailman had been successful in making a snowshoe trail over the 26 miles. So we chartered a horse and, with one man leading the animal and another holding back on the rope to prevent the sled from running up on the horses' heels as we went over the big drifts and down the grades, we succeeded in making the 26 miles in just 10 hours. Our service in that snow blockade netted an attendance of 18 people and the inquiry, "Why on earth did you come?"

We were well repaid when two weeks later the same congregation turned the figures around and made it 81 people, so that, after all, we are convinced, again and again, that we get out of life just about in proportion what we put into the task.

No man's head aches while he is comforting another. *(Indian Proverb)*

LOST RING

During a wedding ceremony I had told the groom to "Take this ring and place it on the third finger of your lady's left hand." He fumbled and dropped it down an open grate register. I whispered to the maid of honor, "Give me your ring," and we proceeded with the ceremony. After the wedding we took a 12-inch pipe off the furnace and secured the wedding ring. Ever after during a wedding ceremony we always saw to it that a rug was placed over an open register.

I have waited more than once for folks to drive many miles for a wedding license or a pair of rings they had forgotten. I have had many beautiful weddings and some sad ones.

For years I have closed my weddings by describing a painting of Holman Hunt's, called "The Shadow of the Cross." It is a painting of Jesus with bare feet standing among shavings in the carpenter shop. The day's work is done and Joseph is putting the tools away on the crude shelves. There is a little eight-inch opening for a window in the western wall and the evening sunlight is streaming through. Jesus is tired from the work of the day. He yawns with outstretched arms and the sunlight streaming through the western window falls across His outstretched arms and makes the shadow of a cross on the eastern wall. Mary is kneeling in the door wondering what this can mean to her boy? Of course the application is that the nearer you live beneath the Shadow of the Cross the better the journey will be.

After this I always say, "And now if you don't kiss her, I will." This dries up tears and sends everyone away in a good mood.

WHEN I SEE THE CROSS

Someone gave our young daughter a luminous cross, thinking she would enjoy its glow at "lights-out time." She was pleased and decided to hang it on the end of the pull-chain of her bed light. "Now," she said, "when I see the cross I can find my light."

Her remark remained with me as I thought, "How true!" When we see any situation in the light of the cross, we can more easily find our way.

We see Jesus as he walked the common ways with man. We follow as he went about doing good. But it is not until we see him in the shadow of the cross, with all its significance, that we really begin to comprehend the depth of his love.

"Never shall the cross forsake me, Lo, it glows with peace and joy."

Prayer: We thank thee, our Father, for the challenging life of Christ who is our light and our salvation. May we walk faithfully in thy light, Amen.

"I am the light of the world: he that followeth me shall not walk in darkness, but shall have the light of life."
—John 8:12

Mildred Pound

I believe it was John Wesley who said, "Some people have only enough religion to make them uncomfortable."

APPENDICITIS

I well remember the night when I was due to hold a service in Grand Marais, Michigan, on the southern shore of Lake Superior. Before this anticipated service, I was at the home of Mr. George Butler, the Grand Marais High School superintendent, enjoying my evening meal.

Unexpectedly, a boy rushed into the house and excitedly called, "Mother wants you to come over right away and see a sick boy. She says you should come before you go to church." I reluctantly pushed away the dessert of bread pudding and went with the little fellow.

After I saw the boy, a big fellow of 16 or 17, I suspected that his problem might be appendicitis. (Of course I did not really know. I must have surmised it because I had been raised with a doctor.) I gave Mr. Butler's boy a quarter to take this message throughout the little community, "There will be no church tonight. The preacher is taking a very sick boy to Marquette, to the hospital."

Next I explained to George Butler that he should arrange to have the boy packed in ice, ready for transportation to the hospital. My job, I told him, was to hold the Duluth Night Express, Number Seven, which was due in Seney, Michigan, 26 miles away, in 40 minutes.

When I reached the depot in Seney, the headlight of the train was bearing down on us, from the east. I asked Mr. Harold Olson, the operator in the depot, for an order to hold Number Seven for 20 minutes to help us get this sick boy out of Grand Marais. He sent the message by telegraph and signed the order 30/30 which was the number of my railroad pass. The conductor from the train who was in the depot talking to the operator said to him, "Why is the signal against us? We are on time." The operator replied, "Just a minute! We are getting an order."

The operator replied, "Here it is. Hold Number Seven until Doten's patient arrives." This order for indefinite extended time was what saved the situation. We had to wait 40 minutes for the patient to arrive.

The passengers from the train were more than a little impatient. What were we doing stopped out in this wilderness? some asked. Others used language that was definitely not Sunday School talk. But, the train stood still.

While we were waiting for the patient, we went to a little hotel, rented a cot and a blanket and telephoned the doctor at Marquette, Michigan, 90 miles away, to have someone ready with an ambulance.

When the patient arrived, he appeared to need surgery so badly that I just rode, with him, in the baggage car.

After the surgery had been performed the doctor said to me, "Preacher, that Grand Marais boy had no chance in the world had you not found him. His was a ruptured appendix."

The case did not close quite that simply. In a delirium the boy got out of bed, before the stitches were healed. He had to have some stitches redone. In spite of it all he lived and went back to his Minnesota home. (In fact he was a long, long way from home because he was visiting a cousin when we found him in this emergency situation.)

Of course not everybody knew the story. Some people complained because we had been bold enough to cancel church, after they had waited two weeks and looked forward to attending church on Thursday evening. Two people wrote the Bishop and complained because we cancelled church. There are times when you just have to ask yourself the question, "What would Jesus do?"

"In all thy ways acknowledge him,
And he shall direct thy paths."

A CHURCH OR TWO

On Saturday we would come into Marquette from the east on Number Seven and at four o'clock, walk up the hill a good half-mile to the place called "Home" to us. The children soon discovered that they had a dad. After frolicking with them, we had an evening meal, then it would be the mail-reading. After this was answered, we had a bath and caught the *Duluth Night Express* westward at one o'clock in the morning. We climbed off the train at exactly four o'clock in the morning at a little town called Ewen, 50 miles east of Ironwood. We trekked to a hotel and slept until eight o'clock in the morning. The Ladies Aid paid for the room and the hotel gave us a good breakfast.

A small church had been built about the time the Diamond Match Company took out the big white pine with which to make little matches. This church was poorly constructed, so much so that we had to discontinue ringing the bell for fear the vibration would cause the church to collapse (but it was in this little church that I heard a good soloist sing "Whispering Hope" for the first time.) There was no question in the world but that we needed a new church.

A lumberman by the name of Jensen died, but he left our little church the sum of $5,000.00 which was a lot of money back in the depression days. I just let it go for a couple of years until everybody really wanted a new church. Then one day I went to see Mrs. Jensen. About the first thing she asked me was, "Mr. Doten, when are you going to build the new church?" Then she added, "My husband left you the money."

It was here I said, "That is just what I came to talk to you about. I sort of had a vision that if you could give us $4,000.00 to go with your husband's $5,000.00 that would give us $9,000.00 to work with and instead of building it of wood and painting it white we could build it of beautiful brick and you would have as much money in the church as you paid for the monument marking Mr. Jensen's resting place in the cemetery." She said, "Who told you that I paid $9,000.00 for that stone monument?" I said, "Oh, a little bird." (It was the undertaker, but he had to live in the town.) I said, "This would be a great investment to generations yet unborn."

The next 12 minutes were the longest 12 minutes I ever lived, because she put her head almost in her lap and never looked up. When the 12 minutes were gone she raised her head and I said to her, "Well, what about it, Mrs. Jensen?" She came back with, "Oh, I was trying to think where I could pry $4,000.00 loose, but soon as I find it you shall have it." (Her nephew was president of the bank and he stood right behind me and we did not talk to *anyone* else until we had that money deposited in the bank!)

I had a pass on the *Duluth South Shore* and the *Atlantic Railroad*. Because of the pass, the railroad hauled the gravel and brick for the new church at half-rate. The brick came from Green Bay, Wisconsin. Those brick were what were commonly called "Rosebush Blend." There was only one other building in all the Upper Peninsula made of these brick and that was in the city of Hancock, in the Copper Country. I went to Green Bay, Wisconsin to order the beautiful brick and I said, "Ship them to G. A. Gustafson at Ewen, Michigan." He replied, "You don't mean Gustafson, the contractor at Iron Mountain?" I said, "That's the man, only bill them to Ewen," and the man came back with, "Gustafson is the 'whitest' contractor in Michigan."

Having a pass, I went to Duluth to pick out birch lumber for trim. The salesman said, "Preacher, you are going to pay an extra $20.00 a thousand if you are just going to take the *pretty* boards." I said, "We will pay." This church was a piece of artistry for a little town. The sanctuary was to the east and a good community room westward. There was a partition between these two rooms that had two doors that rolled right up into the ceiling just like an old-fashioned rolltop desk. By doing this we could open up the area and have plenty of space for funerals. The basement had everything in that day, even steam tables, and was a great community center.

This church was called "Ewen Chapel" and was built during depression days when men worked for 35¢ an hour and begged to work 10 hours. The art glass windows in this chapel were made by Ford & Foreman of Minneapolis, Minnesota and were most beautiful. Today, Highway No. 28 runs past this church. It will pay you to stop and go in. It will be worshipful just to you and God.

One summer day in 1879, A. M. Chesbrough paddled up the Tahquamenon River searching for white pine. By the time they had paddled about 15 miles, they came to the Lower Tahquamenon Falls which they portaged around. Another six miles and they came to the big falls of the Tahquamenon. (The largest falls in northeastern United States between Niagara Falls in New York and the Falls of St. Anthony.)

This was a tremendous portage. By the time they had camped and paddled and paddled and camped for about 75 miles of river somewhere near Newberry or McMillan, they went inland and found the white pine for which they were searching.

The result was that a very large mill was built at the mouth of the Tahquamenon River and a town sprung up called 'Emerson.' You might possibly find a few foundation posts there today. This was one of Michigan's big mills where the logs were sawed into lumber after they had been floated down the Tahquamenon. The dangerous jams of logs were untangled by river drivers with calks in their boots so that they could ride the logs.

In 1927 we were assigned as "Methodism's Sky Pilot" of the Upper Peninsula. This was the missionary work in the 15 counties north of the Straits of Mackinac. We started preaching in a tar papered dance hall, in Hulbert, Michigan. After two years folks had a little change of heart and the town hall was painted three coats of white paint,

136

someone made a homemade pulpit and some downstate church sent us an organ in a piano case. We worked here three more years before we built the church.

About 1931, the State of Michigan surveyed a road into the Big Falls of the Tahquamenon and we secured the right to take the big spruce timber out of the surveyed right of way. These were beautiful straight spruce trees and we only took the better ones. Finnish craftsmen peeled these logs and dressed them down with drawknives so there was no big or little end. In other words, they dressed them to the same diameter. We used short bents in building so that way we used shorter logs which demanded less dressing down. These logs were hollowed out on the top between two chalk lines four inches apart. Oakum, with which you calk ships, placed in that concave top, sat the top log in a groove in the log below. Calked this way with oakum the building was as warm as a passenger coach.

The church was begun with a campaign to raise a "Mile of Pennies." Sixteen pennies make a foot. The children, of course, took this literally and brought in their 16 cents. Ten feet meant $1.60; 150 feet meant $24.00. In little cloth sacks, in paper checks, they came from Oregon to New Jersey, from Minnesota to the Gulf States. Every mail brought more. Everyone in the little town of Hulbert had written to almost everyone they knew and the miracle happened. A mile of pennies is $884.80. When we had something over "Ten Miles of Pennies" (during depression days) we were well on the way because hundreds and hundreds of dollars of donated labor went into this artistic work of love.

Sol Freeman, an enthusiastic sportsman, after finding several dead deer, tossed a few forks of hay into a clearing and a fund was established to feed the deer in the deep snows of winter. Freeman said, "If we can raise money to feed the deer I guess we can furnish a decent place for the kids to attend Sunday School."

The window seats in this Tahquamenon Chapel are made of split logs on wooden pegs. The pulpit is a section of a large spruce log and the top of knotty pine. The Baptismal fount is also an upright spruce log in which a maple bowl is placed. The bowl was sent to the Houghton College of Mines and lined with native copper. The ceiling is of select knotty pine.

The altar in this chapel is in the eastern end and the auditorium seats are reversible, made in oak, so that on occasion they can face a large stage in the western end of the building. A beautiful fireplace has been built in the middle of the back of the stage with a wine-colored traverse curtain that closes off the stage in time of worship unless there is a funeral at which time the curtain is opened and chairs are placed on the stage like a balcony to service seating of the crowd. The windows are made of beautiful art glass. The portable preacher, as he was known, made four trips from Marquette to Kenosha, Wisconsin to help engineer these reversible oak pews. It took two men to turn them, but they were absolutely the same whether they faced the altar or the stage.

The Finnish craftsmen who worked on this chapel were artists in wood. The outside of these logs were finished in spar varnish and are so maintained to this day. A great wide stone chimney and tower combined carry the smoke from the furnace and also the bell in an arched opening.

If you are driving M-28 about 35 miles west of the Soo, turn north a couple of miles to the village of Hulbert (originally called Tahquamenon) and see this pride of woodwork. It is seldom, if ever, locked, and is called the "Beautiful Little Church in the Big Upper Peninsula."

(And by the way, there is a collection box there too.)

EWEN CHAPEL, EWEN, MICHIGAN

TAHQUAMENON CHAPEL, HULBERT, MICHIGAN
THE LITTLE CHURCH IN THE BIG U.P.

HOW TO NAME A TOWN

Seven families went into the woods closely together and hewed out homes. They were in this locality quite some time without knowing what to call their settlement. To get a majority to agree on a name seemed an impossibility. Finally, in 1882 a doctor came into the new community by the name of French and they all met in his home to somehow work out a name for the new settlement.

The first letters of the eight families was suggested and after much puzzling over the problem they came up with the name GERMFASK. This was the first letter of the eight families in the following order: Grant, Edge, Roat, Mead, French, Ackley, Shepherd and Knaggs.

About the same time that Germfask was named a railroad was built from Seney to Grand Marais, 26 miles north on Lake Superior. Then this railroad was extended eight miles south to Germfask. The new railroad was named the "Myrtle Navy," the trade name of a popular smoking tobacco of that day . . . What the Myrtle Navy did was get the white pine to the "Big Shining Sea Water" to be sawed into lumber to help build Chicago. Leon Czolgosz, an anarchist who later assassinated President McKinley, was a laborer on this railroad named the Myrtle Navy. The daily logging train had one passenger coach attached to give rail connection north so travelers from Grand Marais could take a boat anywhere on the Great Lakes.

Forty-five years later the railroad had disappeared and the old grade became the highway of the region. It was then that I was assigned as "Methodism's Sky Pilot" of the Upper Peninsula. The district superintendent said to me, "Alvin, you go into Germfask once and if you never go again I do not think anyone will ever blame you."

During the logging days, a church had been built but was never finished. They did get some plaster on the ceiling

140

but the walls still had just the lath exposed. There was a potbellied stove and a lot of stovepipe. My first visit to this town was on a Friday. I found broken windows and the steps to the church gone. Five young fellows heard that a preacher was coming to town so they caught a young cow and put her in the church. Having been raised on a farm we led the cow to the door and twisted her tail and out she went, steps or no steps! (No animal can stand that tail twisting.)

We cleaned the church, built a fire and rang the bell. Folks came looking to see where the fire was, but four of them came to church. We sat around the stove and had a little service.

Before five years had run their course we had a beautiful little white chapel with carpet from Marshall Fields in Chicago. Twice a month we came into Germfask on a Friday night and held a service. This being but one of the 14 places to which we ministered every two weeks.

I do not believe our Catholic friends had any plaster on the ceiling. Anyhow, they had built too large for the small settlement so they tore their church down and rebuilt it right around the corner from ours. They hauled stone 40 miles from Lake Superior and lay these stone up with black mortar and built a very beautiful chapel. At any social event carried on in the Catholic Church, the Methodist women served the meals and when the Methodist folk had something going on the Catholic women did the work . . . and this was long before we started talking about doing ecumenical things together.

After some time I said something to one of the leading ladies at Germfask about a communion service and she said, "Mr. Doten, it has been 30 years since I have seen a communion service."

We went fishing and when the fish did not bite we took our lunch sack and drew the first draft for a folding communion outfit that contained 24 individual glasses, a bottle for the communion wine, a small tray for the bread and when folded it looked like a miniature suitcase. We then painted it aluminum and it became a very practical tool

141

and served people in so many small communities of the Upper Peninsula. When you had served 24 people we would sing a hymn while some girls would rinse and refill the glasses anew, then you could minister to others . . .

This was the kind of a job where you were forever organizing, building and working your way out of a problem. There was great remuneration in this work, hard as it was, (ofttimes by snowshoes), for after a dozen years we left *four* men working where we began.

Mother decided that ten-year-old Kathy should get something practical for her birthday. "Suppose you open a savings account for yourself," mother suggested. Kathy was delighted.

"It's your account, darling," her mother said when they arrived at the bank, "so you fill out the application."

Kathy was doing fine until she came to the space for *Name of Former Bank*. After a slight hesitation, she put down, *Piggy*. *(Central Church Bulletin)*

HIS CHOICE

During a visit to Israel, our group from Oral Roberts University watched evangelist Oral Roberts hand his own Bible to former prime minister David Ben-Gurion and ask him to read his favorite verse of Scripture. Ben-Gurion smiled and sat down against a tree in his front yard. Only the whirring of our film crew's cameras could be heard as Israel's first leader lifted the Bible and turned a few pages.

Then he read: "So God created man in his own image, in the image of God created he him; male and female created he them."

What a dumb favorite verse, I thought. I had expected something more imaginative than Genesis 1:27—something from the Psalms or the Ten Commandments. I grimaced at the cameraman, certain that the hoped-for footage for a TV special was not to be realized here.

Then, in almost poetic cadence, Ben-Gurion explained his choice: "Before we were Americans or Russians, Israelis or Egyptians, before we were Christians or Muslims, Hindus or Jews, before we were any of the things that divide us today, we were men and women created by God. And that is the message of the great religions."

And for us all, Oral Roberts said, "Amen."

—Wayne A. Robinson

Reprint with permission from the November '78 *Reader's Digest*.

TWELVE EGGS

Four of us fellows went fishing. We had someone drive us perhaps 30 miles, then we walked about 3 miles into the creek. We knew we had 12 miles of creek to fish before we would come, just before dark, to the Jackson camp, where our driver would pick us up.

There were four of us: Alfred, Harry, Billy and Alvin. Each of us carried some of the lunch on our backs. I remember, I had the coffee, the sugar, and the two-quart tin pail in which to boil the coffee. One had the sandwiches, another cookies. Billy had a dozen hard-boiled eggs.

We had to fish fast, passing one another every few rods because we had 12 miles to go. Alfred said, "Today we test the preacher. We don't eat until he hollers." This far upstream the fishing was good. There were plenty of speckled trout, so you just kept the good ones. About two o'clock we came to a little stream about ten inches wide that came tumbling into the creek. There were a number of evergreen trees here so we had plenty of shade. Here it was that Alfred said, "Preacher or no preacher, here is where we eat."

All along the seven miles we had traversed we kept seeing egg shells along the bank. When we stopped for lunch Billy had one hard-boiled egg left, so we made him eat the twelfth egg, too. Somehow Billy did not want any lunch.

For about a mile the creek broke down into 10 or 12 very small streams across open plain where not even grass would grow. Between two of these little streams was a big hole that looked like an open well, about one-third full of water without any inlet or outlet in late summer. I just happened to see a fish rise and take a big bug in this hole-like well. I dropped my line in that hole and took out four of the largest speckled trout I ever saw.

HARD PRESSED

Here is a set of instructions for the Sheldon School in the Dakota Territory back in September of 1872.

1. Teachers will fill lamps, clean chimneys and trim wicks each day.

2. Each teacher will bring a scuttle of coal and a bucket of water for the day's use.

3. Make your pens carefully. You may whittle nibs for the individual tastes of the children.

4. Man teachers may take one evening each week for courting purposes or two evenings a week—if they go to church regularly.

5. After ten hours in school, the teacher should spend the remaining time reading the Bible or some other good book.

6. Women teachers who marry or engage in other unseemly conduct will be dismissed.

7. Every teacher should lay aside from his pay a goodly sum for his declining years so that he will not become a burden to society.

8. Any teacher who smokes, uses liquor in any form, frequents pool halls or gets shaved in a barber shop will give good reason for suspecting his worth, intentions, integrity or honesty.

9. The teacher who performs his labors faithfully and without fault for five years will henceforth be given an increase of 25¢ a week in his pay providing the board of education approves.

Here's hoping you get the raise?

—Unknown

You can't beat the undertaker and you can't fool God.

*　　*　　*

Marriage is no big thing. . . . It's a lot of little things. *(Unknown)*

*　　*　　*

A friend is one who knows all about you and still loves you. *(A. J. Vance)*

*　　*　　*

If we're all sinners, how come I'm the only one who has to stand in a corner? *(Church Bulletin)*

*　　*　　*

A sound discretion is not so much indicated by never making a mistake as by never repeating it. *(Bevee)*

*　　*　　*

Bargain: Something you cannot use, at a price you cannot resist. *(Milwaukee Journal)*

*　　*　　*

When Hoover was president, he gave all his salary back to the government. The idea caught on and now they've got all of us doing it. *(Motor North)*

*　　*　　*

My father said, "If a man gets the best of you, that's his fault, but if he gets the best of you the second time, that's your fault." *(AD)*

*　　*　　*

To make a living, you and I work, like most people. Not musicians, they play. Nor doctors, they practice. As for judges, they just sit. *(Boyd - Detroit Free Press)*

BUFFALO

The American Indian had a dream world! He had magnificent timber, beautiful mountains, oceans of grass and lakes and rivers teeming with fish. And, he had buffalo. Our early settlers pushing to the west would often see buffalo as far as they could see—just a black moving mass. They were likened to fish in the sea.

The buffalo gave the Indian good meat, hides for clothing and covering for his tepee. (It was not uncommon for buffalo hide to be 12 feet across.) Often their canoes, rugs, robes, moccasins, and clothing were made from these same buffalo hides. Buffalo teeth became a rattle for the babies to play with. Bones had a double usage. They became either playthings for the children or they were crafted into tools or weapons. Sinew was used for sewing and binding.

These plains Indians lived very well. They were some of the most healthy people that ever lived. Their diet was mainly fish, deer and buffalo. The Indian name for the buffalo was "Tatonka." Is it any wonder the Indian did not want to welcome the Caucasian, with his rifle?

The "White" man destroyed the buffalo, by the thousands! Not until the herds of buffalo were almost extinct did the Indians begin to give in and give up. (In addition to destroying buffalo, the Indian was also hurt by the "White" man's attempt to subdue him by applying the use of "firewater.")

The buffalo, which were so valuable to both races, stood about six-feet high. They would often weigh more than a ton; the female from 1,000 pounds to 1,500 pounds and the bull from 1,500 pounds and up. In place of a depression which cattle have, the buffalo has a big bump, on top of his head. A cow has 13 ribs, on a side, or a cage of 26 ribs. The buffalo has a cage of 28 ribs. Buffalo live and reproduce three or four times as long as cattle do. Most buffalo live from 20 to 40 years. Cattle have some trouble calving, but not the buffalo. Unlike cattle or humans, the buffalo almost never loses a calf. A young cow generally gives birth to her first calf at two years, but the buffalo does not bear until the animal is three years old. The buffalo has stocky legs and very large eyes. When a buffalo calf is born he is red for about six months. Then he turns brown and black. Dried buffalo droppings were called chips. (These "chips" were the fuel used by the pioneers on their way westward, across the prairies.)

The buffalo milk is said to be richer than that of a Jersey. A buffalo will not overeat. He will run to keep warm. Buffalo always graze against the wind and will survive a blizzard that would wipe out a herd of cattle.

"Buffalo Bill," William Cody, was a frontiersman of the American West. He drove a mule as a messenger and was also a Pony Express rider. His amazing skill with a rifle earned him the name of "Buffalo Bill." He took a contract to supply meat for the men building the railroads westward, across the plains. He completed his contract with the railroad men by killing four to five thousand buffalo in eighteen months. For years he served as a guide for buffalo hunters. He finished his career as a showman.

First, he played in a "Wild West" show, a theater production. Later, along with others, he formed a "Wild West Circus." For years this toured the United States and parts of Europe.

Wild Bill Cody, or "Buffalo Bill," has helped us restore our memories of those magnificent buffalo, an animal that is slowly coming back today. Gerald and Frances Oleson, and their sons, Gerald, Jr. and Donald, of Traverse City, Michigan, are helping to promote the return of the buffalo. Gerald Oleson, or Jerry's, first adventure with buffalo was to purchase ten animals from the Wichita Wildlife Refuge Cache, Commanche County, Oklahoma. Here the buffalo roam among the big boulders of their refuge just as they did before the "White man" came into

148

Oklahoma Territory. This Wichita Wild Life Park covers 59,200 acres.

Each year since the Olesons first purchased buffalo they have increased their herd. Today, they have 231 buffalo on their ranch at Traverse City, Michigan. On their 1,120 acre tract near Engadine, in Michigan's Upper Peninsula, they have 43 more buffalo. This family has five supermarkets. I have no idea how many buffalo they have butchered for market. Buffalo meat is richer and sweeter than beef. If you have not eaten it, you have missed something. (What's more, it is low in cholesterol and fats!) Buffalo meat has from 25 to 30 percent more protein than beef.

Jerry started in business June 15, 1926. That same year he took to himself a bride, Frances Deering, by name. In over 60 years of service in the ministry I have served in many fields and learned to know a multitude of people. Never, in any area in which I have served, have I ever known any couple who have given so much of themselves, so unselfishly, to the community in which they worked and lived. To the churches, to the Northwestern Michigan College, to the folk in need, Jerry and Frances Oleson and their sons, Gerald, Jr. and Don, have given. They have given so much of themselves to the people around them that they really must have a heart full of satisfaction due to their service to mankind.

I will never forget when, following surgery, after I had been released from the hospital, Jerry Oleson came with a large basket of fruit. He stood at the foot of my bed and kept repeating, "Preacher, Preacher . . . I just had to come to see you tonight." After hearing this three times I said, "Jerry, why not the hospital when I was there? Why here, at the parsonage?" He came back with, "Twenty-five years ago tonight I was married in your front room. Frances is waiting out in the car now for me to take her out to our anniversary dinner."

This year's Barbecue 1979 was the twenty-fourth Barbecue, sponsored by the Olesons for the Northwestern Michigan College. The total number of meals served was

320,359. The proceeds to date total $383,161.00. This figure does not include the matching funds for which Northwestern Michigan College Barbecue dinners have qualified. It is believed to be the largest, most successful fund-raising event ever staged for a Michigan college. These meals are served by: the Wigwam Club, the Northwestern Michigan College Faculty, the administration, the student body, the secretarial, clerical and custodial staffs. Jerry and Frances Oleson and their sons furnish all the food for these Barbecues. The only exception is the soft drinks. These are furnished by the Coca Cola Bottling Company.

To give you some little idea of the magnitude of this year's venture, this year's menu is printed on the following page.

150

For your dinner today the Oleson family of Traverse City purchased, donated, and helped prepare and serve the following menu . . .

14,000 STEAKETTES

Cooked outdoors and served on buns with a barbeque sauce made from a special recipe of the Olesons'

4,500 lbs. BAKED BEANS

Prepared from the following recipe:

1,400 lbs. of beans
14 gallons of molasses
28 gallons of ketchup
280 lbs. of brown sugar
210 lbs. of bacon
4 lbs. of dry mustard
2 lbs. of pepper
30 lbs. of salt

RELISH TRAYS

90 gals. pickles
20,000 celery sticks
20,000 carrot sticks
20,000 cheese squares
14,000 Home-made dill pickles

CHEF'S SALAD

COLE SLAW

POTATO SALAD

With 110 bushels of potatoes

120 lbs. of coffee　　　　　　*8,000 servings of milk*

14,000 CHERRY ICE CREAM SUNDAES

Soft drinks: Courtesy Coca Cola Bottling Company

GERALD AND FRANCES OLESON

THREE GOVERNORS I HAVE KNOWN

WOODBRIDGE N. FERRIS

When Woodbridge N. Ferris was a boy in school he was not allowed a slate for fear he might draw pictures. He had plenty of hard knocks in his early life, but by rigid determination and discipline, he became an overcomer. At age 12 a local teacher inspired him to get ready for a life of educational service.

At 16, he entered an academy 8 miles from home. He and his roommate had trouble with some stovepipe and he said, "Edward, why do you never get mad?" And Edward said, "I can't afford it." They were invited out to tea. Napkins and butter dishes were unknown and Woodbridge said, "This was life's greatest embarrassment."

At age 17 he passed a teacher's examination and found employment in a country school. He offered to teach a week for no charge and he boarded around. After this he entered the Otsego Academy in the county seat 18 miles from home. From this academy he passed an examination that would have admitted him to Cornell University without further examination. Then came the Normal Training School. He was always fascinated by preachers so he took a course in public speaking.

At one time he began a medical course at the University of Michigan with no thought of practicing medicine but that it might be of help in his teaching. He returned to New York state and soon found himself principal of his old academy. I have been told that he never allowed a pupil under the sixth grade to use an arithmetic text. This developed a keen mental alertness.

Woodbridge married Frances Gillespie, an early school-day sweetheart, and together they spent a life of teaching. They organized the Freeport Business College in Freeport, Illinois.

For years he had in mind the founding of an industrial school. He finally narrowed the location down to Fargo, North Dakota, Duluth, Minnesota or Big Rapids, Michigan. At last he chose Big Rapids, Michigan, where he organized his industrial school in 1884. At the opening he and his wife were the teaching staff and the school opened with 15 students.

The school was built in 1898 and in 1900 the name was changed to the present "The Ferris Institute." The school now maintained 16 departments and folks trained at the Ferris Institute bore the mark of thoroughness.

Perhaps the most outstanding factor of the Ferris Institute was the School of Pharmacy which became known far and wide and turned out many distinguished pharmacists. You will meet men who were trained in this School of Pharmacy most any place you go. The Ferris Institute has grown into the Ferris State College and today the enrollment is between 10,000 and 11,000.

Over a 25-year period Mr. Ferris lectured in almost every city and village in Michigan, and in nearby states. The Ferris Institute was an awakener, you might say. It was an example of what persistent effort will do.

In 1912, Woodbridge N. Ferris was elected governor of Michigan and re-elected in 1914. One of the greatest tasks of his leadership was his handling of the strike in the Copper Country in 1913. He called in the National Guard of 2,565 men to cope with a very wild situation that had developed, after a strike that had lasted 80 days. In 1922, Woodbridge N. Ferris was elected to the United States Senate.

As a boy, my teacher and I would travel many miles with a horse-and-buggy to hear Mr. Ferris give a lecture, and the thing that lingers in my mind the most about this man was the way he could conclude a lecture by saying,

"I would rather have a hollyhock on a shingle while I am living than a room full of flowers after I am dead."

154

CHASE S. OSBORN

Chase S. Osborn had some rough times as a boy, generally walking for transportation, piling lumber and as roustabout in a print shop. He tried almost everything. He said he did not know anyone could be so deeply in love. He had to wait until the girl was 18 to get a marriage license, and they were married by a Methodist minister. Chase gave his wife a 5-cent bouquet and paid the preacher $2.00 down and $3.00 on the installment plan (and I believe they took their wedding trip on a streetcar drawn by horses).

Chase Osborn ran a newspaper at Florence, Wisconsin, where he began prospecting for iron ore. When he left Wisconsin, he sold his newspaper for $10,000.00 (a lot of money in that day). After Wisconsin, Sault Ste. Marie became his home. Before long he was publishing the *Soo News*.

At one time he was State Game and Fish Warden, then Railroad Commissioner. His Soo paper gave him the means to spend about half of his time prospecting for iron ore. He would walk and carry a pack considerably over 2,000 miles between spring and snowfall, carrying a frying pan, tin tea pail, flour, pork, tea and salt, no sugar though. In his prospecting work Chase Osborn always seemed to have used an Indian and a white man familiar with the territory he was exploring.

One of the ways in finding iron ore in those days was that the compass would not behave. It would often turn a complete circle because of the magnetism of the iron. Osborn spent about half of each year sleeping on a bed of balsam boughs. I believe that his quest for iron ore took him into every continent in the world.

In Chase's succeeding years he was in most every mine in the Lake Superior country, including the Menominee and Gogebic ranges. Once when Chase was seeking financial aid of someone to develop a property he had prospected, and while he was out to lunch, the chap wired a successful Duluth iron man: "Does Chase Osborn know what he is talking about when he talks iron ore?" The wire came back: "You can go sled-length with Osborn!"

The Chapin mine in Dickinson County is, I believe, a good example of a prospector's findings. It was mined to a depth of 1,520 feet and shipped 27,506,868 tons of iron ore. (Folks with money would pay Chase $500.00 a month and an equity in whatever he prospected so that before he died I believe he gave away something over $16,000,000, about half of which was donated to the University of Michigan for research.)

Chase Osborn had a great sense of right and wrong. He tried hard to lead people to choose the right and leave undone the wrongs of life. Osborn had a tremendous personality that radiated leadership. He was an honest politician and had a magnetic personality that radiated power. When he was governor of Michigan he often called special sessions of the legislature to care for some special item that he knew should be taken care of. I suppose you might well call his term of office a special program of legislative reform.

Chase Osborn was often termed a "Crusader." His governorship was a very efficient administration. He was the kind of governor that no institution ever knew when Chase would show up at their door. World iron-seeker that he was, you might well have called him an international citizen. Back in the 30s he was talking about a bridge across the Straits of Mackinac.

Three things that Chase Osborn said that I shall always remember: "Iron is more important than wheat, there are substitutes for wheat, but not for iron ore."

"There should be no government competition with private enterprise."

156

"I would build power plants at the mines and move the power and not the coal."

Osborn spoke to all kinds of groups, often to religious conferences. I have always evaluated Chase Osborn as the most intelligent and best informed man I have ever known.

A missionary was coming home from Africa on furlough. She said to one of her helpers, "I'll bring you back something from America."

The helper said, "Oh, bring me a set of teeth just like yours."

The missionary replied, "I could not do that. They would have to take a cast of your mouth and be fitted."

"No, no!" he said, "I took them out of your glass last night and tried them, and they are just right."

WILLIAM MILLIKEN

Bill Milliken said that his great achievement in the army was to learn to take down a 50-caliber machine gun and put it together blindfolded. His plane was hit and so was Milliken. He was carried from the plane to the hospital while three of his crew were killed.

Bill Milliken always seems to have a vision of great opportunities and he had the convictions to carry them out. Yet, he is a man who can laugh at himself. A very good friend of ours, Don Gordon, was Milliken's right-hand man for years. Gordon had an excellent sense of humor and was a very valuable man.

In 1953, Bill Milliken, along with our preacher son, Donn, was with other young people in an exchange program, when, I believe, they spent 75 days in West Germany. One night in Bavaria, they wound up in a little town where folks declared they had never seen an American! They checked into their inn, observing a peculiar odor, and soon learned that their room was in the outside wall of a brewery, with the vat in the center. The owner was also mayor of the town and back of the vats were the living quarters and then the barn was attached. I believe they had five bands that played on into the morning as a celebration for the Americans. At five o'clock in the morning even guests were awakened to go to the barn to see a calf born. The calf was named "America." The band struck a tune! Naturally it was "America," and the folks went home.

But Bill and Donn had to be on a bus at seven o'clock in the morning en route to another town. They were assigned to be entertained at some army officer's billet. When they knocked on the door and someone answered he said, "Donn, how did you come to be here?" and Donn replied, "Dick, what are *you* doing here?" Dick had been an usher in his church back in Lake City, Michigan.

As a young man, Bill Milliken was altogether too good-looking for a man and still is. Doubtless, three of his top fields as Lieutenant Governor were economy, mental health and education. He was pretty much a promoter of scholarship programs for high schools. He sponsored the bus law which provided transportation for children in parochial schools, as well as being a backer of released time for religious instruction. I believe this was as much as two hours a week.

In his days in the Senate before his governorship, he would persistently try to work out solutions to problems and he always had the courage to back up his convictions. While he was Lieutenant Governor he made some such remark that "Lieutenant Governors were like spare tires, necessary and important when an emergency occurred." Wherever you find Bill Milliken, there is always excitement and a challenge. He made it so! I can just hear Bill saying, "Folks do not want a spare tire governor."

Governor Milliken has great respect for other people and their ideas. Milliken is a man very much in control of Bill. He has a quiet persuasive manner that men and women respect. He marshals his facts with great diplomacy. When something new has to be presented, Bill Milliken has the conviction and courage to do so. He has an inquisitive mind. He is always looking for information with which to enrich Michigan. When you consider Governor Milliken's leadership, he is a man who very much does his own thinking and then follows it up with tremendous courage. There was a day when Milliken was pushed from many directions to run for the United States Senate, but quietly said "NO," then used that big smile. I can hear Milliken saying, "I can make a decision, then live with it."

William Grawn Milliken was Lieutenant Governor with Governor George Romney. When Governor Romney resigned to accept a post at Washington, D. C., Milliken was elevated to the governorship. He served out the two remaining years of that term and has since been elected to three terms as governor of the state of Michigan, making him four times governor of this state.

159

It's not fair to tell of Governor Milliken and not his brown-eyed Helen, the Denver girl who became such a tremendously helpful wife and devoted mother. (Even if they did have to set five wedding dates!!!) That's what it is to be in the service of your country and finally come through with a purple heart and a good wife who sees one important task in her life—to help her husband succeed.

When Bill chose his Helen Wallbank, he sure drew a premium. Every real man needs to marry twice, one time to the best girl he can find and one time to his job. That is exactly what Bill Milliken did for Michigan.

I hope you don't need to keep up with Bill, because he *runs* most of the places he goes . . .

My grandmother and my mother were both Smiths. They always reminded me of the traveling man who was going into Chicago on a train when he saw a sign, SMITH MANUFACTURING COMPANY. Right away he said, "I always wondered where they all came from."

GOVERNOR AND MRS. WILLIAM G. MILLIKEN

PARTIAL DESCRIPTION OF A BOY

"After a male baby has grown out of long clothes and triangles and has acquired pants, freckles, and so much dirt that relatives do not dare kiss him between meals, it becomes a *boy*. A boy is nature's answer to that false belief that there is no such thing as perpetual motion. A boy can swim like a fish, run like a deer, climb like a squirrel, balk like a mule, bellow like a bull, eat like a pig, or act like a jackass, according to climatic conditions.

"He is a piece of skin stretched over an appetite. A noise, covered with smudges. He is called a tornado because he comes at the most unexpected times, hits the unexpected places, and leaves everything a wreck behind him. He is a growing animal of superlative promise, to be fed, watered, and kept warm; a joy forever, a periodic nuisance, the problem of our times, the hope of a nation. Every new boy is evidence that God is not yet discouraged by man.

"Were it not for boys, the newspapers would go unread, and thousands of picture shows go bankrupt. Boys are useful in running errands; a boy can easily do the family errands; with the aid of five or six adults. The zest with which a boys does an errand is equalled only by the speed of a turtle on a July day. The boy is a natural spectator; he watches parades, fires, fights, ball games, automobiles, trains, boats, and airplanes with equal fervor, but not the clock. The man who invents a clock that will stand on its head and sing a song when it strikes will win the undying gratitude of millions of families whose boys are forever coming home to dinner about suppertime.

"Boys faithfully imitate their dads in spite of all efforts to teach them good manners. A boy, if not washed too often and if kept in a cool quiet place after each accident, will survive broken bones, hornets, swimming holes, fights, and nine helpings of pie."

—Author unknown

I recently purchased a wig from a mail-order house. It arrived with this note enclosed: *Due to the possibility that this wig may slip off your head, do not wear it to bed. Many husbands have been frightened by the sudden awareness of a strange, furry animal under the blankets and have been known to damage the merchandise.*
(Barbara Cabet)

FORD FAMILY CAR

The mechanic who worked on my car worked for the Ford Garage in Marquette, Michigan. (I believe he later became the well-known shorter man of the *Amos and Andy Radio Team.*)

This mechanic was working one day on a Lincoln car with a custom body. I came along and stepped up to talk with him. As I did so a gentleman said, "Just step back, please . . . "

I answered, "What is this, *Henry* Ford's car?"

"No," said the mechanic, "but it is *Edsel's!*"

It was fun getting this close to the best custom job the company was capable of coming up with.)

Every summer the Fords came to Marquette in a railroad pullman. At the depot, they were met by their security guards and their private cars. Like a wind, they were whisked away to the Ford summer home in the Huron Mountains. Their time was spent in retreat and relaxation. Only occasionally did they come to Marquette to a matinee. This particular day that I remember they were attending a matinee while their car was being worked on. One dramatic correction needed was to find a way to release the horn which was stuck.

The mechanic who knew me said, "Stick around, preacher. I am going to take it out soon for a test run. We will take a ride."

In retrospect and even then I guess, it was not the short ride in the car which pleased me and stayed with me . . .

It was the popcorn and apple cores on the floor of the car.

Why, it was just like Doten's car!!!

MISSING THE BOAT

One evening, I went to the Newberry Post Office around five o'clock and purchased eight air-mail stamps. On reaching home, I discovered that the seven stamps I had left had an "air-o-plane" printed on them, but that the air-o-plane was upside down. (Knowing nothing about the value of improperly printed stamps) I sputtered about the designer of this particular stamp. I used six of the stamps and kept one for many years until it became so soiled and shopworn that I used it also . . .

In the 1970s I picked up a newspaper and read that one of these stamps had just sold for $35,000.00!

I never felt too badly about it because I felt God had a hand in it. Had I kept the stamps I doubtless would have left the ministry. God had something left for me to do. The priceless stamps did not contain the glue that kept the letter of my life together. (A recent newspaper informs me that the bidding on this same stamp is now between $60,000.00 and $80,000.00.)

While I was supplying a church in Kalkaska, I stopped one day to have lunch with the funeral director. I discovered that he or a friend of his had some connection to the men behind *Kentucky Fried Chicken*. During our luncheon together they revealed to me that they had just made a worthwhile investment in a new issue of *Kentucky Fried Chicken* at 40¢ per share. One of the wives said to me, "What do you think of our investment?" I answered, "You can't go wrong when you can get in on the ground floor of anything that folks eat!" Then I added, "If I can scrape up $1,000.00, I will see you tomorrow about this."

The following day, I worked all day calling on homes, the hospital and hunting up new folks and was 14 miles (half-way home) when I thought of the *Kentucky Fried Chicken*. I slammed on the brakes to turn, looked at my watch and it was half-past 10 o'clock so I said out loud, "Oh, I'm too old to bother with this, go on home."

At 40¢ a share that $1,000.00 I was considering investing would have purchased 2,500 shares. Around eight months later when the stock in *Kentucky Fried Chicken* reached $75.00 a share, these men said, "Sell!" and next day it sold for $80.00 a share, I believe the top it has ever known.

You can figure it for yourself, 2,500 shares at $80.00 a share would have meant something to a preacher-man about ready to retire, but evidently God still had something left for me to do?

Following this I did purchase some *Chef Pierre* stock. (To me *Chef Pierre* is the maker of America's best pies.)

Immediately, the company went on strike, so I guess the Lord intends to keep me humble?

Seated in a crowded bus,
A thing that I despise
Is to see a lady stand—
That's why I shut my eyes.
(Modern Maturity)

CORNISH DELIGHT

About 11 o'clock you would see the wives of the Cornish miners heading toward the tipple of the mine with their husbands' dinner buckets in hand. These buckets with their man's number on each one would be placed on the cage and taken down the shaft to the level on which their husband was working that day. Each lunch bucket contained a real hot pastie and few Cornishmen would eat their pastie without singing the doxology for grace.

RECIPE

The big secret of a good crust is to use about two cups of finely ground flour, add water until dough is right. Now divide into six equal parts. Take 1½ pounds of good steak and 1 pound of lean pork, cut both into cubes about 3/8 of an inch square, ½ dozen ordinary potatoes sliced, cut 2 onions fine, add about a cup of rutabaga, few carrots cut up, add butter to taste. Now roll out each of the six dough parts so they are about the size of a pie tin. Place a sixth of the mixture on one half the dough then double the other half over and crimp the edges, so you have something that covers half a pie tin. Make some holes in the top crust; put two of these on each pie tin; place the three tins in the oven and bake 1 hour at about 350 degrees. This makes a delicious hot meal until you will have no room for dessert. The above directions should care for six hungry men.

When you ask a Cousin Jack (Cornishman) what a pastie is, he would say, "Why, it's a root house surrounded by a Cousin Jack," and a Cousin Jinny would be his wife.

HOW TO GET RID
OF A MINISTER

1. Look him straight in the eye when he is preaching, and say "Amen" once in awhile. He'll preach himself to death in a few weeks.
2. Pat him on the back and brag on his good points. He'll work himself to death.
3. Start paying him a living wage. He's probably been on starvation wages so long he'll eat himself to death.
4. Rededicate your own life to Christ and ask the preacher to give you a job to do. He'll probably die of heart failure.
5. Get the church to unite in prayer for the preacher. He'll become so effective some larger church will take him off your hands.

—Bishop Gerald Kennedy

By Permission

COMPLAINT BLANK

Concerning your minister and your church

Give description of complaint in this space

☐

Write distinctly

GIVE FULL DETAILS

—Unknown

TATTOOED LADY
OF THE TAHQUAMENON

One morning I went into an Indian C. C. Camp located between Newberry and Sault Ste. Marie, but some miles north toward the Tahquamenon River. The officers in this Indian camp were all Caucasian. It was our privilege to eat with the officers.

When we came to the table, who did I meet but Kendrick Kimball, Roving Editor for the *Detroit News,* a man I had known for years. Mr. Kimball introduced me to a companion by the name of Smith.

Mr. Kimball said, "Preacher, I need you tomorrow. I want you to take me to the Tattooed Lady of the Tahquamenon. Three months of the year she lives down river in a shack. The other nine months she is with the circus. Her entire body is covered with tattooes." My answer was, "I cannot go tomorrow because I am starting with my good wife for Rochester, Minnesota, to seek help from the Mayo Clinic."

Mr. Kimball came back with, "But Preacher, there is $20.00 in it for you." I replied, "My wife is worth more than $20.00. We'll get Dr. George Swanson's chore boy to go with you. He will go for $5.00."

Then it was Kendrick Kimball turned to me and said, "This man across the table from you who I introduced as Mr. Smith is really Dr. McQuigan from the Whitney Building in Detroit, Michigan. He has spent 15 years with the Mayo's before he went on his own. He works diligently for six weeks; then he plays for ten days. He is out here "playing" with me now. Get out your notebook. I am certain this doctor man will give you some good leads on what to do when you get to Mayo's."

170

I finished with quite a list of good tips. Finally, Dr. Mc-Quigan said, "Now, knowing a good surgeon will be of help, I am certain. First, ask for Dr. Judd. Then ask for Waltman Waters and Howard Gray." (Waltman Waters, one of the the great surgeons at the Mayo Clinic, married a daughter of one of the Mayo brothers.)

On our journey to Rochester, Minnesota, we met a cousin with whom we had previously corresponded but never met. Alma Doten met us in the depot of St. Paul or Minneapolis. With the wife in a wheelchair we were served hot meals, on trays, by this cousin whom we had never actually met before. She was an angel of mercy at that time and for the rest of our lives.

When we arrived in Rochester I was amazed at the ease with which my names and notes from Dr. McQuigan expedited our registration and preliminaries.

After four full days of examinations and tests we found ourselves in a room with our redheaded lead doctor, whose name we cannot recall, and two other men. One of these men was holding an X-ray plate that showed two gall stones, one the size of a 50-cent piece, the other the size of a quarter. The man holding the X-ray plate said, "Preacher, if we had these two stones out we could shake dice!"

"Preacher, who would you like for a surgeon?" he asked. I answered, "What does a backwoods preacher know about surgeons? I know you have dozens of them and a couple thousand nurses." It was at that point I queried, "What about Dr. Judd?" The doctor said, "You want Dr. Judd? If you want Dr. Judd you can have him but you will have to wait a week. He is in Chicago lecturing at the Presbyterian Hospital." At this information, I said, "What about Waltman Waters or Howard Gray?" The lead doctor responded, "This country preacher knows where he is going." He turned to me and said, "Preacher, shake hands with the man who is holding the X-ray plate. This is Waltman Waters. Now shake hands with the other man. He is Howard Gray. If you want these men, you may

171

have both of them." (And I believe Waltman Waters made the incision and Howard Gray did the work.)

My wife, Iva, stayed in St. Mary Hospital about 21 days. Our entire stint in Rochester, Minnesota extended to about 31 days. In the meantime I became well acquainted with Howard Gray. I would wait for him to leave surgery so that we could have lunch together. (It might be two o'clock or I might nearly starve as I sometimes waited until four o'clock to eat with him.)

On the day of our dismissal I went to say good-bye to Dr. Gray. He came to the door in his surgical uniform. I asked him, "Do I have the story right? Was not your father president of the Union Pacific Railroad?" "Yes," he answered. "Was not your brother superintendent of the Omaha System?" Dr. Gray came back with, "Yes, but how on earth did you learn this?" I then told him, "If you are going to be a good preacher you have to be a good detective. Gray, just how did you miss being a railroad man?" Dr. Gray said to me, "Preacher, I was railroaded to death. We had railroads for breakfast, dinner and supper. I grew up wanting to be a good Christian surgeon." He stretched out both hands to me and said, "Preacher, these are Christ's hands. I can't walk on the water. I can't raise the dead. But, just as far as I can go these are His hands. When I cannot practice surgery in that spirit, I do not want to be a surgeon any longer."

We corresponded for years. He was an outstanding man—one of my unforgettable people on life's highway—who lived to help serve mankind.

> Christ has no hands but our hands
> To do His work today
> He has no feet but our feet
> To lead men on His way,
> He has no tongues but our tongues
> To tell men how He died
> He has no help but our help
> To bring them to His side.

What if our hands are busy
  With other work than His
What if our feet are walking
  Where sin's allurement is?
What if our tongues are speaking
  Of things His lips would spurn?
How can we hope to help Him
  Unless from Him we learn?

—Annie Johnson Flint

Used by permission of Evangelical
Publishers, Toronto, Canada.

When our twins were little, I would take two wash-basins, set each youngster in a wash-basin, take their two little feet in each hand and pull them swiftly over the carpet. When I was completely out of breath, they would both be saying in concert, "More, Daddy, more! More, Daddy, more!"

THE LEADING GOOSE

In our travels as a free-lance missionary for the church in the Upper Peninsula of Michigan, we still hung on to our Indian followers. One of the high spots of the year was the 10 days that we spent at Zeba, (meaning "Little River" in Indian,) probably the largest Indian camp in the Lake Superior region. The forenoons were spent by the Chippewas in fishing and hunting, in season and out of season. These people felt that they had the inherent right to what God had placed in nature. The conservation department seldom interfered as fish was a top item on their diet.

The Ojibways generally spent the afternoon in gambling of one kind or another. They used cards and dice on blankets, on the ground. The cards and dice were some sort of a contest with bones of animals. Evening was church time. There were hundreds of these Chippewas from Northern Minnesota, Northern Wisconsin and Northern Michigan. Their services were held out-of-doors with planks across logs for seating. The speaker's platform was made of rough lumber. It had a covering or shelter at the top, a roof-like protection from the sun. There was a crude pulpit gleaned from some abandoned church. There were a couple old church pews for the choir and a couple of chairs for the chief, and the speaker.

The congregation generally sat on the planks across the logs arranged in two big rows with the men in one row and the women in another. The men usually sat at the speaker's left. The meager collection was taken up among the men. The women collected babies which they offered for baptism. Theirs was usually a generous offering.

If your discourse was not plain and simple, one by one they would start slipping away. You had better make it short, or soon all you would have would be the choir—if, luckily, they stayed?

174

The last night of this annual session proved to be a dismal failure. We began to wonder wherein we had failed, for our Indian peoples had always been so responsive to us. This service was an eight-minute sermon and a benediction without a hymn.

With the benediction, the whole woods took on life! It seemed that from behind every bush and every tree there was life about to appear. They cleared away the planks and the logs and hundreds of Indians, many with their feathers, came from all directions. After a very enthusiastic dance, they were quiet and quiet reigned as only it can in an Indian group.

The chieftain rose on the platform to inform the preacherman that after all they loved him and had decided to adopt him into the Chippewa tribe. He said, "We love you. We take you into our family, our own flesh and blood, Ojibway Boy. From tonight your name shall be Negonasah."

We whispered, "We do not like the name." He wanted to know why? We then reminded him of the two mining towns close together on the Marquette Range—Ishpeming meaning "heaven," in Indian and Negaunee meaning "hell."

"No, no, no," said the chief. "Negonasah, means the Leading Bird."

The next morning we stepped off the train at Marquette at seven o'clock and went up the hill to home and breakfast. We told our story of the new adoption—rather puffed up at being the "Leading Bird." Mother looked up from the other end of the table and said, "Daddy, we have known around here that you have been the 'leading goose' for a long time."

WE HAD THE CASH

Back in the days when our parents lived, whenever they became ill, they were not cared for in a nursing home. The children just naturally inherited the job. Children felt that they owed this to their parents and they loved caring for them. Thus it was that Grandmother Doten lived with us for a dozen years. When her time came to go she died in our home in Newberry in Michigan's Upper Peninsula. We took her to Standish for burial in the Lower Peninsula of Michigan.

At the time of Grandmother Doten's passing, I phoned Ernest Pierce, president of the Union National Bank at Marquette, Michigan and asked him to send me a draft for $200.00.

That evening I was at the post office awaiting the sorting of the evening mail. The postmaster asked me to sign for a registered letter. When I opened the letter, just a little later, at home, I found $400.00 in cash, in small denominations. I sputtered all evening about the president of the bank, Ernest Pierce, sending me $400.00 in cash, instead of $200.00 in a bank draft. I sputtered silently. I did not phone him to ask why.

The following morning at nine o'clock, not a single bank in all of the country opened. Then it was that I understood why I had received double the amount that I had requested and why I had received it in cash.

About half-past nine the same morning, Jess Barrett, a mill operator, came to the home. He brought me another $200.00 in cash.

Thus it was that the traveling preacher had $600.00 in cash to take his mother to her final resting place, when no one, anywhere, could cash a check or get into their bank box.

176

I can still hear my mother singing:

> "O, come angel band.
> Come and around me stand
> Bear me away on your snowy wings
> To my immortal home."

Teacher: Why are you late?

Boy: A sign I saw was to blame.

Teacher: What does a sign have to do with your being late?

Boy: It read, "School ahead—Go slow."

(Central Church Bulletin)

RED OAK

'Twas a late summer day. Friend wife and I were cruising along in a V-8 some northern parishioners had given us. We were north of the AuSable River in territory that I had fished 30 years before. The trees, then about my height, were now at least 30 feet tall and so thick you could not see through them. A maze of narrow sandy roads ran like spiderwebs through the pines. Suddenly we came to a place called "Red Oak."

You sort of came on Red Oak as an accident. It was not easy to find because it was scattered among a meshwork of trails in the AuSable State Forest. There was a low building rented by the state of Michigan as temporary headquarters. Back under the pines was a long building originally used as a stable but later used for cars, trucks, tractors and other state equipment. One section of this long building was used as an ice house. Between this building and a home, stood a gas pump. There was also what you might call a water deck or platform that held a long row of large cans filled with water in case of fire. There was a small store nearby and up on Elk Hill stood a tall fire tower. This was Red Oak, but you never could see it all at any one time.

All these trees reminded me of some of the big trees of Michigan. The largest white pine tree today in Michigan is down the Keweenaw Peninsula near Copper Harbor. This pine is 19.25 feet in circumference and 6.08 feet in diameter. But Michigan's big white cedar is located about three miles east of Mio on the big bend on the south side of the AuSable River and is approximately 12.8 feet in circumference and almost four full feet in diameter. The largest group of white pine trees in Michigan is the Hartwick Pines, seven miles northeast of Grayling.

Somewhere I read not long ago about the largest white pine that ever grew in Michigan. It grew near Mio—the Red Oak region just north of the AuSable River. The article said this tree was 200 feet in height, 34.6 feet in circumference. This would mean that this same tree would have been 11 feet in diameter and this was a big tree for this country. Evidently this huge tree was destroyed in the big fire that swept this region in 1911.

There were so many sand trails going in every direction from Red Oak that we were baffled. We told the ranger that we felt we were pretty good woodsmen, but in the last 30 years the pines had grown tall and the roads were many, that we would like to get to a lake not too far from there, then over to the rapids on the AuSable River.

The ranger went into the cabin and brought out a brown paper bag which he slit with his knife, then, using my car hood for a table, he drew a very exacting map of the region. Having finished this he said, "How long do you expect to stay in here?" I replied, "About four days." We fished the lake and caught nothing. We went by Mr. LaGuire's map, about seven miles to the rapids on the river, and had a splendid catch of brook trout. (Any fisherman's prize!)

It was on the fourth day about one o'clock when we returned and he said, "I'm glad to see you." When I asked to buy five gallons of gas someone spoke up and said, "We are only supposed to sell you one gallon to help you get out of here, but you are a preacher so we will sell you *two* gallons." We were grateful, thanked them and went our winding way.

Years afterward when we were serving Asbury Church in Traverse City, Michigan, a mother and her two children came to church one Sunday. After the service they lingered around near the door, finally the lady said, "We are new here and we heard your son preach in his big church, but decided we wanted to hear the father too, before we settled on a church." Mother LaGuire then said, "We would like to have you come to dinner. I think there is enough chicken in the pot if you have no other plans." I checked with my friend wife, then told this mother, "You ought to know better than to offer anything like that to a *Methodist* preacher man!"

At the dinner table Carlos LaGuire sat at my left and I kept listening to his voice and looking at that black hair. Finally I said, "Mr. LaGuire, did you ever work for the Conservation Department?" He said, "Yes, I did . . . " Then I told him the story of long ago when I was baffled as to which way to go in the woods and a young man drew a map for me. I kept watching for a reaction but there was none until I had finished the story. He was silent. He slowly laid down his dinner tools, looked me straight in the eyes, as a big grin spread over his face. Carlos LaGuire said, "You have your man."

This developed into a very fine relationship and I later had the joy of drawing this man a map by which to live. I baptized him, and later took the whole family into membership on the same Sunday.

For years Carlos LaGuire had been the labor relations man for his company and had negotiated the contracts. This was a nerve-wracking job and he came to Traverse City, Michigan, for a few months of rest. He then was sent to the company's Philadelphia, Pennsylvania, office. Here he faithfully attended a men's Bible class and also became the leader of the church-sponsored Boy Scout Troop.

After a few years he was returned to the plant in Wyandotte, Michigan. Soon after he developed cancer and left us for a better country. The pastor, also a minister from the Mission Board in New York, and the writer had the funeral. It happened that I drew the meditation. I told the people that day how this man drew a map to keep me from getting lost in the woods. How the Good Lord led him to Traverse City so that I could draw him a map by which to live.

These are *some* of the compensations that come when you work for the "King of Kings."

180

TRANSPORTATION

I now live where I can see the big planes come in over the blue waters of Grand Traverse Bay. Not far away I hear and see the engines that take the "big birds" up into and beyond the skyline. These planes are heading from this northern resort center to all sections of this great land. Big oil boats come in and out of the deep harbor here. Sailboats are raced here. The wind whirls them by. Family and company yachts sit silently at the shoreline—not more than a few hundred yards from my Hill Top Manor. It was not always so.

As a child I remember our mode of transportation was something right out of Paul Bunyan's "Big Blue Ox" tale. Our mode of transportation, however, was not a myth. It was the truth.

My father had one large, calm, big white ox. You never reined an ox. You just talked to him. Often Mother and I would ride on the dray as father walked and talked to the ox, Old Lou. If you made a clucking sound with your mouth and teeth, he would go. When we called "whoa," he would stop. If you just walked beside him and kept talking to him it was not all that difficult to keep him moving. I was so tiny that it was difficult to stay on his big broad back. (That is why we rode on the dray.) I recall that the ox had long white horns with an inch of brass on the ends. This one ox was not only the helper but the only means of transportation for four families who cut new homes out of the woodland. All of the men worked together. They took turns cutting timber and clearing land, purchased for $2.50 an acre.

Later on, my father purchased a more skittish animal, a big bay horse. For a long, long time I was afraid of the horse. My mother would ride on a dray, holding me backwards, so that I could not see this fast moving horse.

Transportation was a far different story when I was grown and a free-lance missionary for the churches in the Upper Peninsula of Michigan. I had a pass on all of the railroads north of the Straits of Mackinac. This included the *Duluth South Shore* and *Atlantic,* the *Soo* line and others. On your travels you always carried your belongings in a backpack. You did this because you could not carry a suitcase. Your arms had to be free so you could swing them. This kept the circulation going enough to keep you from getting frostbite. The pack that you carried on your back had a small round tincan with white shirt collars rolled tightly. You wore homemade black sateen shirts with a collar band. This way you could have a clean white collar every morning. (These were often called the portable preacher's 1,000 mile shirts.) The backpack also contained a flashlight, simple Sunday School supplies and a sweater. You learned to leave everything at home—unless you absolutely had to have it to get by. You slept in your sweater instead of your pajamas. You wore that same sweater under your coat if you were riding on a load of logs. In extremely cold weather, the driver of the horses would build a fire on top of the load of logs. This only charred the bark. It did not harm the lumber inside. This way you kept your hands warm when it was 30 below zero outside.

When I could get across the country where I had to go no other way I resorted to snowshoes. One community that I serviced was 26 miles from the railroad. I snowshoed these 26 miles a number of times when I had to go into Grand Marais, Michigan, from Seney. Grand Marais was on Lake Superior; but, Seney, Michigan, was an old lumber town on the railroad. Making this trip was difficult for any traveler so an old abandoned house had become known as the Halfway house. One room which had been an office in lumber days had an old bed spring in it—but no blankets, of course. There was nothing to do but sleep in all of your clothes including your overcoat. This same room had a little two-foot box stove with one leg and three bricks. You maintained a fire from pine roots left in the room. You always chopped roots in the cold of the morning and left them for the next traveler.

A lone-wire telephone system ran through these woods. The priest, the doctor, the mailman and the portable preacher paid for the telephone in this old Halfway house.

If you were stranded in a blizzard there was a certain method of reaching the outside world. You took a wire, coiled on a big spike, across the road and grounded it to an old iron pump. Then you kept ringing until someone answered, 13 miles either way, in Seney or Grand Marais. This one wire system was your contact with humanity. It kept rescue parties from going out to hunt you if there was a heavy storm.

The floor of the office in this Halfway house had egg shells and dirt about two inches thick. One thing that you soon learned to carry was plenty of stick candy in your pack. Oranges, sandwiches or apples would freeze. Stick candy never froze and it gave you energy enough for those quickie meals.

Reverend Marshall Reed, who later became a Methodist Bishop, heard me tell this story on the air—during a radio broadcast about the mission's work in the Upper Peninsula of Michigan. For years he sent me boxes of *Sanders* stick candy. He did not, however, say who was sending it. I discovered, inadvertently, who the anonymous donor was. One day the Bishop and I were visiting while his good wife was filling out Baptismal certificates. He stopped talking long enough to sign his name. Watching his signature, I then discovered who was the "candy man."

I said, "Now I know who it is who is sending me candy."

He replied, "I thought that you would never find out."

I wore out one pair of snowshoes on these northern trails. A second pair was stolen while I slept on the train. After this happened I asked a "half-blooded" Indian who was very clever with his hands to make me a pair of ladies' snowshoes. I am very small and these light snowshoes helped me to spread my weight and kept me from sinking in more than a half-inch.

It was an Indian who really taught me how to use snowshoes. He said, "Just play that you are drunk. Swing your body and the shoes so that the shoes do not interfere."

Talk about transportation? There was a man by the name of Spencer who lived in Grand Marais, 26 miles off the railroad on Lake Superior. This man bought from a government outlet an air-o-plane motor for $100.00. He built a strong but light sleigh, mounted it on skis and installed this motor. This contraption was a hog for gas but could it go!

One day this man set out to take the preacher to Seney on the railroad. Everything went well long as we were on the road through the hardwoods, where the snow did not drift. Once we were out on the plains we could not find the trail for huge drifts. These plains were dotted with huge pine stumps. Out of the road the front axle hit the top of one of those stumps hidden by snow and the driver and the preacher kept on travelling. We must have gone at least 40 feet. I have always been so thankful that we came down in deep snow and not on top of one of those pine stumps.

When I was a little fellow and the school-teacher boarded with my mother, she was always saying to me, "Alvin, you will make a man yet before your mother." This I just could not understand.

A GIANT AMONG MEN

In June, 1953, our church held its annual conference in Bay View, just north of Petoskey. Inasmuch as I was close to the Burns Clinic in Petoskey, I made an appointment with Dr. Burns' nurse for him to give me a medical examination preceding surgery.

The appointment was for late afternoon and as most appointments are made a month or six weeks in advance I, on short notice, was, of course, placed at the end of the day. After waiting two hours I said to the waiting room nurse, "Dare I go get a sandwich?" And she said, "I would not if I were you because if Dr. Burns calls you and you are not here he will not wait." It turned out to be another two hours before I was called. When I was ushered into his office he said, "Preacher, I knew you were out there, but if you wanted to see me badly enough, you would wait." Then he said, "I have had a terrific day," threw himself into a big chair and said, "let us relax and visit a little."

The walls of his outer office were covered with photos of leading doctors from all over the world. As we visited I walked around looking at the men, a few of whom I happened to know . . . I said, "Why, there is Waltman Walters," and a little later, "and here is Howard Gray." (both Mayo men). "Well," he said. About that time I spotted a portrait in light pink with the word "Flemming" in the lower corner. So I said, "Is this Alexander Flemming of penicillin fame?" And he said, "Yes, it is." I said, "You doubtless know the story about Flemming and Winston Churchill?" This time he said, "No," whereupon I said, "You are a very busy man, you don't want to listen to my stories," and he came back, "Before we go any further I want to hear this story." (He had a long day and really wanted to take 'in sail'.)

I told him how, when Alexander Flemming and Winston Churchill were boys, they went swimming together. Churchill had cramps and Flemming pulled him out. The following Sunday the Churchills had young Flemming over to the evening meal. During that meal they asked him what he was going to do when he grew up and he said, "I want to be a doctor. I haven't any money but somehow I am going to be a doctor." The result was that the Churchill family paid for Flemming's medical training. Years and years afterward when Flemming was experimenting with his molds he used some of his experimental penicillin on Winston Churchill when he had double pneumonia and saved his life a second time. By this time the tears were running down Dr. Burns' cheeks and I had unknowingly made a lifelong friend.

Doctor Dean C. Burns was born in the family home in Petoskey, Michigan, December 12, 1896, because there was no such thing as a hospital around. In high school days he became the office and chore boy for doctors John and George Raycraft. He delivered medicine, gave vaccinations, did laboratory work and helped in so many ways.

He attended the University of Chicago and the Rush Medical College. While in medical school he did laboratory work, taught nurses, worked around the hospital at anything that needed doing to help obtain a medical training. I believe his classmates were Charles and William Mayo. After graduation the two Mayo brothers tried hard to persuade him to join them in founding a clinic at Rochester, Minnesota. He said, "I like the idea but I want to go back home and do this very thing for my town." He returned to Petoskey and entered practice with the Raycraft brothers who had started him off as an office boy.

By 1931, both of the Raycrafts had died and Dr. Burns inherited the work of three men. He also inherited a rickety wooden hospital plus unpaid bills. Despite all the new responsibility, Dr. Burns believed the time had come to do more than plan for a clinic. He began by recruiting Dr. William Conway, an eye, ear, nose and throat specialist. These were depression days when few men could envision

186

anything new, but Dr. Burns had a strong faith in what lay ahead. Men with his determination do not give up a real dream easily. At a card game four women decided to give $1,000.00 apiece as a beginning for a new hospital. Mrs. Coleman induced a banker to head a campaign for funds. The banker soon learned that the hospital and clinic had been more than dreamed about. That lot by lot over the previous years, the land had been acquired for the site of the hospital and clinic. The latter being founded in 1931.

The banker, with his friends, raised $75,000.00 then organized another campaign that netted $200,000.00, so that, by 1939, the new hospital was opened with 68 beds. Over the next few years Dr. Burns built the clinic staff. By 1938, Dr. Burns had secured Dr. Benjiman Blum (I believe the First Assistant in Internal Medicine at Mayos). In 1942, Dr. A. J. Hegener was added to the staff as a Urologist. Dr. Weburg joined the clinic in 1945. These were all medical leaders who laid a great foundation, until today there are 72 specialists serving in this clinic. Today, the Burns Clinic and Little Traverse Hospital are often spoken of as "Little Mayos." Today people come to the Burns Clinic from other states, from Calgary to Toronto and you actually have to say to yourself, "One man made it so."

Dr. Burns was dreamer, organizer, builder and chief of staff until 1961, then director emeritus. It would almost take a book by itself to enumerate the medical awards given him. He not only organized Little Traverse Hospital and the Burns Clinic, but also the Burns Foundation which helped to make possible so many worthwhile ministries, the North Central Michigan College being one of them. Dr. Burns was admitted by election to a Fellowship in the Royal Society of Health (Great Britain), one time Counselor International College of Surgeons. The University of Chicago Alumni Association presented him with its prestigious Public Service Award, chosen from Alumni nominees from around the world.

Besides carrying this terrific load he gave 49 years to general surgery. My own life has been richer for having known Dr. Dean C. Burns. I look in the mirror and say, "Alvin, what have you done?"

Today, the successor of Petoskey Hospital and Little Traverse Hospital and Burns Clinic is called Northern Michigan Hospitals, Incorporated and they employ approximately 800 people.

We had been out ministering to fishing villages, mining camps, timber-cutting shanties and came home with a hundred dollars missionary money. Friend wife said, "There is a couple here that want to get married."

I said, "Bring them into the office." I had this hundred dollar missionary fund on top of the pull-out shelf of the roll-top desk. I just pressed the money down and pushed in the board, married the couple, and forgot all about the money.

I went to the bank, borrowed the hundred and sent it to the Mission Board. For six weeks I could not find that money. One night I awoke about two-thirty a.m., sat up in bed and could see myself pushing the money down on that board shelf and sliding it in out of sight. I turned on the light, took a coat hanger and made a hook, and then fished out a ten-dollar bill, went back to bed and to sleep. After breakfast, I took the back off the roll- top desk and secured the other ninety dollars.

THE WHITETAIL

The whitetail deer are found throughout the United States, Mexico and parts of Canada and British Columbia. They are not to be found in Australia or on Madagascar.

Antlers show first as short spikes (I believe in the second year). These antlers start as soft lumps and grow very fast, they are filled with blood vessels and covered with soft hairy skin called "velvet." You will find young trees with the bark rubbed off. This is where the deer have been rubbing this soft skin or "velvet" off their horns. The blood vessels dry up and the antlers harden. They grow anew each summer and drop off around the beginning of the year. Antlers are hard to find in the woods because they are a luxury to porcupines.

The principal deer ranges of Michigan are in the northern two-thirds of the state. When you get above Lake Superior it is primarily moose country.

Deer are the shyest critters there are. They don't want to be seen. Much lumbering increases the herd. They love the tender treetops, and the new saplings that grow up are dessert fodder.

If the winters were extremely mild we would have more deer. Deer will eat spruce and balsam but they are starvation rations. Deer starvation is generally the result of more animals than the habitat can support. The ill and the young lose out because they are shuffled off the trail and out of the way by the more dominant and aggressive adults.

Many of our trees are too big for deer food. The cutting of pulpwood leaves the deer a real feast. The trouble is that he needs other twigs, branches and leaves to go with the aspen because his stomach badly needs a mixed diet. One of the real problems with deer is that they like the farmers' tender wheat fields and his newly-planted fruit trees. Of course they prefer the tender trees to the tough ones. I shall always feel that the big problem of controlling the deer is the food problem, to me far greater than the controlled season. Lack of food supply becomes a law of nature.

As far back as I can remember there has been much fault found with the management of the deer herd, when in reality the big problem is food. Oversized herds and over-browsed ranges are the real issues. I would estimate that 100 female deer would produce 180 fawns each year, but remember—not all these fawns live. A greater enemy of the deer than the wolf or hunter is nutritional deficiency.

Each hunting season there are always a few fatal accidents. Small, I am sure, compared to automobile fatalities. There seems to be some risk in everything even to repairing the shingles on the roof after a storm. Mark Twain once remarked that "Statistics would appear to prove that it was dangerous to get into bed—seeing that most people die there!"

The whitetail deer were probably at their peak in the 1940s. We seem to have a wasteful society. In seasons when we hunt male deer only, we keep finding many does that have been shot and left behind. Some say, "Let nature control the herd" but nature cannot do this in the presence of man. Our fathers hunted for food, but today it seems more for recreation than for food.

Fawns are born in early spring and often nurse until early autumn. Deer are much like humans; they lose their baby teeth at about 18 months. The age of a deer can best be estimated by the wearing down of his or her teeth. In summer, a deer needs a bushel of green leaves and twigs and in the winter nearly the same amount of twigs and buds each day. Acorns are splendid food, but not to be found every season. Deer need a mixture of browse. The one item they might live on alone for awhile would be white cedar. By overbrowsing, deer will kill small food-producing plants, thereby endangering their own life.

Commercial logging operations are a great boon to the deer. This provides tender treetops, then much tender new growth. If you want to feed deer, make it alfalfa or fine

190

clover. If you feed in racks, the larger deer bunt the smaller ones away and get most of the food. If you scatter the clover around over a large area, then the smaller deer have a real good chance to eat. Corn is good but the whitetail often overeat on corn and then die. If I were going to feed I would do so twice a week.

Mills with the great appetite for pulpwood leave abundant food for deer. The deer love the tops of those cuttings. The danger here is that they do not survive well on one kind of cuttings. They so badly need a mixed diet. It is my judgment that when one can go into the woods and count from 50 deer up, there are too many animals for the food on the range. Severe winters are always certain to speed up the decline of the herd on the average. A deer's first winter is always his roughest, 75 to 80 percent reach 18 months with 8 to 10 percent reaching 2½ years, and the remaining 10 percent growing even older.

Someone asked my boy, "If your dad goes hunting will he get anything?" My boy's answer was, "If dad shoots, he will have meat!" I do not want to wound them and let them get away. I want to be pretty sure of my shot or let them go.

We formed clubs on the Eastern end of the Upper Peninsula, especially at Hulbert, to feed the deer. We would buy trucks and trucks of cheap clover hay (timothy is not much use to the deer). We also used cull butter bowls from a woodenware factory in the town and in these bowls we would place cull oats, sometimes with cracked corn. We would feed the deer on the edge of the big swamp along the east branch of the Tahquamenon River. This little town became a showplace for people to come and take pictures.

You follow a beaten path on the edge of the woods in deep snow, in late winter and you will find batches of snow that look like whipped potatoes—dig down here and you will find your dead deer, either the very old or the very young bunted off the trail by strong healthy animals, they are left to dig their own grave, floundering in the deep snow.

Deer can become great pets. I have seen a deer nose around and push open a downstairs bedroom door and then curl up on the bed. He did not care whether it was a spare room or not! I often ate with a family in a hotel kitchen. These folks had a pet deer if ever I saw one. One morning I had put butter and syrup on my pancakes when their pet deer came in suddenly from the *left* and took all the cakes! They gave me a clean plate and I buttered and syruped them the second time and all of a sudden he came in from the *right* and my cakes were gone! (Of course I did not try to stop him. It was just too funny.) Finally I said to the hotel folks, "Just how does a preacher get his breakfast around here, anyway?" They led their deer outside and I enjoyed my pancakes for the morning meal.

One night just before the opening of hunting season I had preached in Hulbert and came out two and one-half miles and swung onto M-28 heading for Newberry when a large deer tried to cross right in front of my Ford. He put his head down, slipped over the windshield and the top of my car and onto a log over the ditch. I never knew whether the bumper or the log broke his neck. But it had no more than happened when a car came over the rise in the road and stopped. The first man out said, "Preacher, what are you going to do with that deer?" (I recognized his voice as the sheriff from the Soo.) I said, "Well, I live right by the conservation headquarters in Newberry and I thought I would take it to them and let them give it to the State Hospital or whatever they wanted to do with it." If I remember correctly his deputy's name was Wilson. The sheriff said, "Wilson, come help this preacher load this deer."

So it was, the sheriff took me off the hook . . .

A PAIR OF JEWELLS

(This story was written by Cornelius Beukema and appeared in the Traverse City *Record-Eagle.)*

There's that line from Gilbert & Sullivan's "The Mikado" which goes "He never will be missed"—a line that has been just one among thousands in Ken Jewell's teaching and coaching and conducting of choral works over the years.

That phrase is especially significant now because, after this summer, Ken Jewell himself will be missed. And so will Mary, his wife since 1935, who is as deeply committed to Interlochen's musical production and overall life as Ken is.

Ken is Dr. Kenneth W. Jewell formally—Ken to his friends and "Uncle Ken" to myriad students who have followed his baton with rapt attention. Indeed he will be missed by all at the Interlochen Arts Academy after commencement June 3 and by those participating in the National Music Camp's golden anniversary season this summer. As usual, he'll conduct the Gilbert & Sullivan operetta, this year "The Grand Duke." It's scheduled Aug. 3 and 4.

The reason: Ken, age 67, and Mary, just turned 65, will be entering the ranks of senior citizens. He will leave his post as director of choral activities at Interlochen. She will depart from her assignment as head resident advisor in Thor Johnson dormitory—for senior and junior academy girls. In summer she has been attendance office supervisor, "a sort of truant officer," she remarks with a smile. They've been in camp since 1949—it's their 30th season—and at IAA since 1964.

But they'll remain close, in the beautiful home they purchased—on the Boardman River—from Ann Landers in 1967. There, instead of helping to shape the lives of students and steer them in the right directions, she'll devote full time to homemaking just for Ken and he will put his very considerable manual talents to full use.

He has applied those talents in putting together a harpsichord, a grandfather's clock, coffee tables, lamps, sewing cabinets, a desk—which she describes as a thing of beauty—other things that require a well ordered mind and skilled hands.

"I do it all in my shop," he says, then adds—a bit somberly, we thought—"I'll be spending much more time out there." Their pastimes will include bird watching, which long has been a joy.

And deer are usually nearby; they saw five on their place a few mornings ago. But he'll fill guest conducting spots, including turns with the Central United Methodist Church choir in Traverse City. He has been conductor for the Northwestern Michigan Symphony Orchestra and was Rotary Minstrel chorus director in 1966-68. And he'll certainly continue practicing a long time hobby as a ham radio operator.

Meanwhile, Ken is usually busy, with his choral work, his teaching of voice and solfege, and particularly preparing for a performance here of the superb group that bears his name, the Kenneth Jewell Chorale of Detroit. The appearance will be supported by the Michigan Council for the Arts.

The chorale—its presentations have been described by critics as outstanding—will sing in the Grand Traverse Performing Arts Center Saturday evening, bringing Haydn's "Creation" to Corson Auditorium, with the Arts Academy Orchestra accompanying and Dr. Jewell conducting.

Once more, such voices as those of Carolyn Grimes, soprano, Conwell Carrington, bass, and tenor Tom Parker—an IAA alum—will be heard. Grimes and Carrington will have an added incentive to be at their peak; they are charter members of the chorale, thus have lent their talents to it for 16 years. Conducting "The Creation" offers Dr.

Jewell a special objective: merging the efforts of Interlochen students and professionals in fine performance of a major work in musical literature. He will appear as emeritus conductor, status which he acquired in 1976.

And this time the chorale will be coming TO Ken Jewell. From the time he organized it, he drove 90,000 miles a year, often three times a week to rehearse the group in Detroit—a 500-mile round trip.

The chorale appearance punctuates what is generally a busy life for the Jewells. It's one of mostly teaching for him, but Mrs. Jewell has the job of helping to keep life running smoothly and efficiently for 160 girls aged 16 and 17. Efficiently, we mention, because those lives proceed at a high level of competence in a school that requires so much of its students artistically and academically.

All of which implies counseling—and more counseling. That's a job the Jewells often share in their dormitory quarters. Counseling permits Mary to be occupied with her favorite hobbies, knitting and needlepoint, as she helps "her girls" solve such problems as are posed by girls of that age.

"Multiply 160 girls by 14 years and you understand why I've done a lot of needle pointing," she remarks. And have the girls appreciated it? The answer: A sign reading "House Mom and Dad" which they have put over the door leading to the Jewells' quarters.

Living as they do, the Jewells can relate anecdotes by the dozen—like the one about that time Ken had prepared the Rackham Choir (he conducted it for 14 years) to sing the Beethoven 9th (Choral) symphony in English with Paul Paray and the Detroit Symphony orchestra.

The soloists, though, had learned their parts in German. "So, I let 'em sing in English," Ken Jewell relates. "The soloists sang in German—and only the critics caught on." He might have told the one about the time he was conducting in Kresge auditorium and suffered a coronary occlusion but finished the assignment on stage before going to Munson Medical Center for a long stay.

Kenneth Jewell attended elementary school in Syracuse, N. Y., moved with his parents to Detroit at age 5, and graduated from Detroit Northwestern High School in 1930. It was at high school that he and Mary Stewart met. He graduated from what is now Eastern Michigan University in 1934 with a bachelor of arts degree in public school music.

His first position was in Romeo where he taught music—grades 1 through 12—for eight years. He worked on his master degree at the University of Michigan in summer, and was granted the degree in 1941. In 1942, the Jewells moved back to Detroit and he took over the band, orchestra and choirs at Pershing High School.

After 15 years at Pershing he was transferred to Osborn High where he set up the music department. The move to IAA came in 1964—and was a natural considering that he'd been on the National Music Camp faculty since 1949. Mary Jewell, born in LaPorte, Indiana, moved to Detroit at age 5, graduated from Northwestern High summa cum laude in 1931 and after her marriage to Ken assumed what she always has regarded as her major role, that of homemaker.

The homemaking role expanded as three daughters were born. They are: Alice Freudigman, Grand Rapids, mother of Karen, Eric, Kurt and Kenny; Carol Frohlich, Indianapolis, mother of Albert and Martha; Lois Swanson, Detroit, mother of Lori and Chris.

So, while Ken Jewell is busy out in his shop, fashioning new furniture, Mary will be needle pointing and knitting and quilting. She has a specific goal: Making a quilt for each grandchild—and, remember, there are eight.

But there will be other things in their daily lives. He'll keep in touch with the world via ham radio. And they'll play chess, using a set he made. Naturally, they'll find a lot of reasons to visit the Interlochen campus.

196

Interlochen Photo, Courtesy of Mary Brill

DR. KENNETH AND MARY JEWELL

THE BIG EAGLE

We folk who live in the Upper Peninsula often speak of that great land as the "Big Eagle." Its beak away down Keweenaw Peninsula, beyond the Copper Country; its eastern wing north of Detroit; and the western wing lacks just four miles of being straight north of Davenport, Iowa. This is a big spread in any man's land. Actually, the Upper Peninsula is a few miles longer east and west than the lower Peninsula is north and south.

The majority of Michigan's wonders lie north of the Straits of Mackinac, Isle Royale in "Gitche Gummee," (Big Shining Sea Water) Lake Superior. Actually a part of Keweenaw County, perhaps the most outstanding of them all (about 40 miles long and from 9 to 12 miles in width), is in itself a National park. Isle Royale has baffled mining engineers. It has miles of prehistoric mining pits that date way, way back. Some archeologists claim that over 8,000 tons of pure copper have been dug from these pits in the lava beds of the island, that the work done there was greater than that required to build the Pyramids. I believe Isle Royale holds the largest herd of moose in America. Greenstones and agates are numerous on the beaches.

The Porcupine Mountains in the northwestern part of the Peninsula are the highest range between the Alleghenies and the Black Hills. The Lake of the Clouds is situated high in these mountains and the largest perch I ever caught were taken from this lake.

The locks at Sault Ste. Marie are the world's greatest man-made waterway, bringing grain, copper and iron to the rest of the world.

Mackinac Island is surely one of Michigan's magnificent wonders.

The Tahquamenon Falls on the river of the same name are the largest waterfalls between Niagara and the Falls of

St. Anthony. These falls are very beautiful and a tremendous tourist attraction.

There was a day when the copper mines of the Keweenaw Peninsula were most outstanding. Some of the workings were over a mile in depth. There was a day when this was probably the most continued string of mining shafts in the world. Telephone communications and railroads, doubtless the greatest underground system known to man. If you were to go back 75 to 100 years, it is said that in those days more children from the Copper Country went away to college than any regions of the United States. This tells us something of the wealth of the community. Over 40 years ago the Calumet & Hecla Mining Company paid out something over $200,000,000.00 in dividends.

There are many grains from which you can make bread, but only from iron can you make steel. In the early development they dug the ore, smelted it and shipped it as pig iron. Today, low-grade ore is made into pellets. This has revamped the industry and made possible the handling of low-grade ores.

As mining opened, up came the Cornish miners from England. Then the Finns came to this north country, as it was so much like their homeland. Other nationalities followed until at one time there were 42 different nationalities in the city of Hancock. The largest Finnish Seminary was located here.

Marquette is the leading banking center, the chemical center and the railroad center. All the Upper Peninsula is like a spider's web reaching out to Marquette.

The largest employment today is timber, and the region is probably growing three times as much timber as it harvests. This speaks well for the tomorrows. Today, there are machines that chew a tree and all its limbs into chips so that chipboard and other items are pressed from these chips. This enables man to use the cull trees and the odd timber and save the better stock for growth.

Tourism is in third place and most likely to expand. The resorters are increasing with winter and summer. You

199

get perhaps four or five days of hot weather during each summer. You have good cool air and always want a blanket before morning. Business will go where people like so much to live. If it's clean air you want, it is north of the Straits.

The Upper Peninsula is larger than Belgium or Switzerland, as large as Massachusetts, Delaware, Rhode Island and Connecticut combined, has 4,000 inland lakes, 12,000 miles of streams and 1,600 miles of Great Lakes shoreline. Surely Mackinac Bridge ("Big Mac"), one of Michigan's wonders, is higher than the tallest skyscraper in the state and I believe ranks with the seven wonders of the world.

The city of Hancock is farther north than Montreal, Canada. Lake Superior (Longfellow's "Gitche Gummee") is the largest fresh water lake in the world. Fort Wilkins, at Copper Harbor, is the only wooden fort east of the Mississippi with its original buildings still standing.

I'm getting toward the end of life's way. Soon I'll be sleeping at Woodmere down at Standish, where in school days I took care of a doctor's horses, gave chloroform and on Halloween helped run a skeleton up a flag pole! When I go to rest there, I'll be on the north side of the lot, four feet nearer the Upper Peninsula, which I loved with all my heart and life's best days happened.

"'Twas truly God's country, especially in October when God spilled His paint pots of Gold."

After dad and I had talked for 30 minutes, he said, "This won't do. I must get to work. This will not buy the baby a shirt or pay for the one that's worn out."

MIDNIGHT SHOCK

Back in 1930, Bishop Nicholson called me down to the Clifton Hotel, in Marquette, to ask me if I was any relation to Frank Leonard . . . He said some of the men told him that I called him "Uncle Frank." I told the Bishop that George Olmstead, who preceded Frank Leonard as superintendent, always signed his name to all of his men as "Uncle George." This simply carried over when Frank Leonard took the district. He replied, "That clears that one up." It was then he told me that he would like to have me take the district. I immediately asked him if he would give me four days to think about it?

Four days later I sent the Bishop a night telegram that read: "I took a vow to go where I was sent and, if you say the word, I will go. But I am only forty, and there will be much jealousy. I am so happy on this missionary job in the 15 counties of the Upper Peninsula. What's more, I don't like the idea of sleeping with 42 Methodist preachers in bed with me every night. Kindly leave me where I am." He honored my request.

While we were riding on a train together, Frank Leonard said to me, "Alvin, I have had both jobs, the pilot's job and the superintendent's, and you have the best job." Thus it was that I stayed on another 10 years, had a tremendous experience and much satisfaction. As I look back at it, I feel it was the best piece of work I ever did. When we try to do what is right, it is then that a power greater than we, a power called "Love," takes a hand.

Doubtless the greatest moment of my ministry came at the General Conference of 1936, in Columbus, Ohio. I had been asked by Dr. Kohlstedt, head of the Home Mission Board, to show pictures of my work as "Methodism's Sky Pilot" at an afternoon session. There were just under

201

1,000 delegates from around the world at this conference, which comes every fourth year.

At exactly midnight, someone rapped on the door of my hotel room. I climbed out of bed and let them in. Who should it be but Dr. Anderson, our minister at Johnstown, Pennsylvania. He said, "Doten, I have a real job for you." "What now?" Then it was he said, "Bishop Richardson was taken suddenly ill and rushed to the hospital. He is now 'under the knife.' The last thing he said was, 'Get that little white-headed man that spoke on the Upper Peninsula this afternoon and have him take my place, giving the devotional address at 8:15 in the morning.'"

In those days General Conference lasted three weeks, so only 20 or 21 Bishops would get to give this morning address. There were around 80 more who might have been chosen, but he asked for Alvin. I did not sleep that night but I was ready by six o'clock. I well remember one thing Dr. Anderson said to me. "Don't go over 15 minutes. If you do they will ring a buzzer on you." So I made it in only 12 minutes. Dr. Anderson told me I did a better job than I had done the afternoon before. And that was as near as Alvin Doten ever came to being a Bishop.

A boy asked his grandfather why he spent so much time reading the Bible, and grandpa replied, "Just getting ready for the last examination." *(Unknown)*

PO-DUNK

When we speak of someone who came from away-out back somewhere, we are prone to say, "They came from Po-Dunk." If we are a bit disgusted with folks and wish them to get out-of-the-way we are tempted to say, "Go to Timbuktu." These were not just fiction, they were real places, one in Michigan and the other in Africa.

Timbuktu actually exists in Mali, about 1,000 miles east of the Atlantic Ocean and approximately another 1,000 miles north of the equator in the big western bulge of Africa north of the Niger River. Timbuktu is on the southern edge of the Sahara desert. Its homes are all one story baked mud construction. It was one of the great centers of the slave trade. Timbuktu was not visited by white men until 1826.

But, Po-Dunk is another story. Po-Dunk was a Michigan town, located in the southwestern part of Genesee County, just north of what today is Lake Fenton. It was actually settled in the early spring of 1834 by Morgan Baldwin and George Judson. Mr. Judson helped Mr. Baldwin build a log cabin, then returned to Oakland County, but came back late the same year and took up a claim for 250 acres and moved his family here in November.

George Judson built a store, a sawmill, blacksmith shop and a gristmill which was run by water power provided by a sluiceway a mile and a half long, dug by hand from Long Lake (now Lake Fenton). The facilities provided the essentials of those early pioneers.

Later, a post office was established at Po-Dunk with Mr. Judson as postmaster. About the same time, Mr. Judson was appointed Indian agent for all the southwestern part of Genesee County . . . This was a real challenge as there were far more Indians living here than white men (these Indians were Chippewas and Ottawas). They received only kindness from their new agent so there was always friendliness between them. For some time women and children were more or less frightened.

The Indians came for many miles to have corn ground at the mill. They often camped for three or four days wrestling and watching the waterwheel. Perhaps a loose shaft or a flat-spot on the grinding stone made the waterwheel seem to keep saying, "Po-Dunk, Po-Dunk, Po-Dunk" over and over again and again so the Indians, charmed by the waterwheel, named the place *Po-Dunk*.

There were high hopes of a railroad, but the surveyors ran it west through Linden and Durand. About this time Judson was lured west by the California gold rush and about the beginning of the Civil War, Po-Dunk just faded away.

A frame house was built (the first in the region) for a trading post with the Indians. Today, a Pioneer Memorial Association has been formed, the house was moved to a better site not far away, to save it from destruction, so that today it has become a real memorial of the pioneer region . . . It is well preserved and cared for, with a cyclone fence around it.

In the new building you will find the steering wheel, life saver and fog horn from the old passenger boat *City of Fenton;* many hand tools, early atlas of Genesee County, old pictures and records and many other artifacts. Among the many things you will find in this Pioneer Memorial Shop is a wooden bathtub lined with copper . . . There was no wood on the bottom so that the water was warmed by two kerosene burners beneath the tub, the oil flowing from an elevated tank. The hours for touring are from 2:00 p.m. through 5:00 p.m. on Sunday afternoon.

It will be time well spent.

LETTER OF INTEREST

We recently received a letter from our good friends, Orm and Madge Danford, former members of Central Church who now live at Williamsburg. They sent a picture postcard of the laying of the cornerstone of the church on August 23, 1912, which we have placed on the bulletin board across from the office. We would like to share part of the letter with you, with their permission.

Dear Reverends, the Brubakers:

Felt the church should have this picture for its archives. It may be too late but perhaps one of your staff could mount this on a poster on your church bulletin board with an inquiry whether anyone can still identify anyone in the picture.

I smile with recollections as I write:

1. The tiny congregation in that big church when we came to Traverse in 1945.

2. The thot that Rev. Alvin Doten (who was Madge's family minister in Norway, Michigan) would have been in his twenties had he been able to attend *this* ceremony.

3. My 20 years as Judge in the city hall next to the church and my first civil marriage—My God (and not irreverently), what would I do?—and scooting across the alley into the morning-quiet, empty church to cop a hymnal and have my court clerk quickly type the marriage sacrament and (then smile again) as over the years I always thot each time there was a marriage: No matter who they were, or where they were from, they *"always got married Methodist!"*

4. Don King who fabricated and helped hang the chandelier from the center of the dome (was that a job!).

5. Frank Purvis and his Sunday School class.

6. The times in the morning when I would have a tough decision in court and could slip over for a moment or two—sit all alone—a few pews back—gazing at that beautiful, bright, serene, stained glass window—and Ed Zimmerman, the custodian, stopped his vacuuming—stood in silence—wondering why I was there—and me wondering too—seeking answers.

7. The times before the church was opened on Christmas Eve (and believe it or not, there was that time)—dark and lonely—and we would get kids ready for bed—in pajamas—bundle them up—load them in the car—the crunching snow—the patient vigilant lonely street lights—drive over to Donn Doten's—borrow the key—and go down all by ourselves to Central Methodist—go in that great dark room—put a little votive candle on the railing before the altar—kneel together with that tiny flame flickering on that big stained glass window—and "have Jesus' birthday." Illusion or not, but we all knew Christ's face just shown! Ask our kids yet.

God bless you and your people and Central Methodist.

—Orm and Madge Danford

(Thanks, friends. Those of us who have been around for awhile will smile along with you. Others will too, we're sure.)

With Permission

Happiness depends upon two assets, which, fortunately, I have: good health and a poor memory.
(Ingrid Bergman)

THE NEXT GENERATION

Some of my memories of the early years were the times we went over the Tahquamenon River north of Newberry where we had fair roads for eight or nine miles then a sand trail until we came to Pine Stump Junction. Here the trail went on north a few miles over the Two-Hearted River and on to Lake Superior. At Pine Stump Junction a branch road turned eastward through some very wild country. The main trail was always marked by a weather-beaten split shingle, pointed on one end and nailed to a pine stump. This told you which trail to keep until, at long last, you came to Pike Lake three or four miles south of Superior's shore.

I remember how we would make our bed on the ground with a rubber blanket over the top to keep off the rain. How that in the morning, we were awakened by some splashing in the water, we would throw off our rubber blanket and the rain it had gathered through the night and watch whitetailed deer swim and play in the lake. After a breakfast of bacon and hot cakes we headed our Model "A" Ford another four miles eastward to the Little Two-Hearted River which was a haven for speckled trout. The big fun of these expeditions was always cooking meals and being out-of-doors two or three days with your boy.

Donn found himself in a normal amount of mischief. I well remember when he came home from school with a bloody nose and some loose teeth. When he was a little older he kept turning out the gas on the stove when his mother was trying to cook the evening meal. Thus it was when I came in off the trail Mother said, "Donn has a licking coming." I took him to the basement where we sat on two blocks of wood and talked. I finally told him, "Had I been your Mother I would have just served the potatoes, carrots and the rest of the supper uncooked. You would have survived on the raw food for once, but with your two sisters on your back, it would never have happened again!" At last I said, "This time I am going to give you the benefit of the doubt, but I'm going to make a deal with you. You lean over the workbench and every time I hit the bench with this strap, you holler!" Soon Mother sent his twin sister downstairs to stop the proceedings and I had to give her a quarter to keep still. It was two years before Mother ever found out what happened.

Donn was small of stature, but he soon developed leadership . . . I well remember when, in his early youth, he carried a speech contest . . . He was an eighth-grader and because he showed some promise he was allowed to compete in a high school oration contest. The judges were not informed that the little fellow was not as yet in high school so awarded him the winner. (Which, of course, he was not allowed to accept because actually he was not a high school student.) I believe it was this same year that he wrote an essay against the liquor business and won in his home county, then in the 15 counties of the Upper Peninsula of Michigan. (If I remember rightly he received a $5.00 check for this, his first winning.)

At Newberry we lived in a three story house and the chimney from the furnace came up through the boy's room on the third floor. In the winter time this was one of the warmest rooms in the house. In this upper retreat a red-headed, freckle-faced boy two years ahead of Donn in high school would coach him in speech. Today, that coach is the Honorable Rex Martin, Circuit Judge at Adrian, Michigan. As a boy Rex always reminded me for all the world of Tom Sawyer. Thus lay the foundation for the victories of high school days, college plays and the like.

One Sunday I had preached in the morning but was just too sick to stay on my feet so I went to bed. About two o'clock in the afternoon I called my son into the room and said, "Donn, there will be 40 to 45 people at the Marks Schoolhouse at 3 o'clock. They will stand around waiting for the preacher man to come. Daddy is too sick but, if you thought so, you could drive the Ford out there. Have the

208

people sing three or four songs, repeat the Lord's Prayer together, read the 37th Psalm (that is a good one of 40 verses), and don't forget to take up the collection. What's more, if you thought so, you could talk 10 minutes." This was a chance to drive the car 14 miles each way. He hesitated a minute and then said, "I'll try."

When Donn returned about two and a half hours later he came into my room and I said, "How did you do, son?" and he replied, "Well, I talked 20 minutes." I quipped, "What on earth did you talk about?" The boy said, "Well, I memorized the signs on the way out. There was a railroad sign that said "SLOW," boats, worms, Chevrolets, tomatoes, potatoes, chickens, etc., until I memorized 26 signs, so I talked on "Signs on the Highway of Life."

I said, "Mother, we have a preacher."

In early November I asked the boy to go into Eckerman (a sawmill town between Newberry and the Soo) and preach on a Tuesday night. The lad inquired, "Where are you going tonight, Dad?" and I said, "Into a lumbercamp." He came back, "Do they know that you are coming?" I said, "No, but they will give me a good hearing." The boy said, "Dad, if they don't know that you are coming, why don't you go with me tonight?" then he added, "Someday I am going to have to do this in front of you anyway, and you are going to have to listen to me, so why don't you go with me tonight?" I replied, "If that's the way you want it, all right, and you can drive the car the 35 miles each way."

There was a large man in the crowd who could not sit in those little seats in the schoolhouse, so he always kept a wooden box in the entry that he would carry in and place in the aisle by his wife, blocking the aisle to other folks. After the half hour opening of the service, I introduced the boy and he spoke for about 22 minutes. When he sat down, this big fellow with a voice like John the Baptist said in his loud voice, "Preacher, it's you for the lumber woods, the kid's got you skinned! Did you hear what I said, the kid's got you skinned!"

That schoolhouse turned into a tumult of joy! It was hard to get order, sing a hymn and bring a benediction.

Two and one half miles from that little sawmill town we turned onto M-28 (the main road from the Soo westward across the Upper Peninsula). The first snow of the season was starting to fall as the lad said, "Dad, I guess this settled it tonight. I think I have to be a minister." Vern Holding never knew what a push he gave the lad that night. It started him on a great journey.

Like all boys growing up, there were times when Dad did not know too much and a certain amount of hostility developed until one day he wrote home saying, "I guess the best times we had together was trout fishing," so he decided to drop out of school for a week and wrote that he would meet me on the Platte River, near Honor, in Michigan's southern peninsula and he added, "We can work on renewing our relationship." It was a great time we had. Even his mother joined us and it had been years since she had been in a trout stream.

One of the mountain peaks on life's way was to see this boy graduate from seminary and then came the great day when, along with the Bishop, I placed my hand on his head to watch him ordained a minister of the Gospel, like his old dad.

The lad had a fine sense of leadership in camping and organized different forms of camps that were used church-wide. He became very interested in the student exchange program between the different countries, so much so that he carried the responsibility for the placing of foreign students in the western half of Michigan. For years he and his wife had exchange students in their home from overseas. This led many people to do the same. If a student did not work out in a home where they had been placed it was Donn's responsibility to find a new home for this student. Most of the students were flown one way and returned the other way, by boat. He and his wife often went on these boat trips with 1,000 to 1,200 students returning to Europe. He would hold a 30-minute chapel service each day on the boat and have better than 700 students in the chapel.

Finally, the different nations worked out a plan whereby someone representing each country met on the French Riviera to work out a program of preparation before a student was exchanged and Donn was the one chosen to represent the United States in the building of this program. Thus, a plan was worked out whereby a student had much the same coaching whether they went from Germany to the United States, from Italy to Mexico, from Denmark to Canada, from Brazil to Spain or from Sweden to Australia. Thus it was that the time spent on the French Riviera was a great investment.

I would say that he made a dozen trips overseas. He was sent to South America on a preaching mission to 11 countries on that continent (I am not so sure but that he was sent to see how the World Service monies were expended?) A couple of work camps trips took him to Alaska and a world emergency found him, in 1971, with a task force in Bangladesh. He seems to have become the family traveler.

For years we were keen competition in different churches in the towns of Cadillac and Traverse City. My boy always played the game. He would say to new folks, "Before you make up your mind which church you want to attend, you should hear my dad in the other church." We tried to reciprocate by telling them to hear the boy before making a decision as to where they would go to church. It was not always easy, but it paid good dividends. We had a slogan: "If you don't like Doten, go to Doten." Each church argued that they had the best preacher, but that was finally resolved when the boy was assigned to the University Church, East Lansing, Michigan.

But he is still my son "Donn" and very gracious to the old man. Some folks call him "Dr. Donn," but his old dad remembers a skinny, sickly kid with a bent fish pole and an excited face. But he grew up and made a 175 bowling average, a lot of years of school, a wife, and two children, one who married another minister to keep this thing going.

211

He drew some very significant church appointments, twelve years in Central Methodist, Traverse City, Michigan; nine years in Trinity Church in Grand Rapids, and now nine years in University United Methodist, East Lansing, Michigan.

He still gives the old man a hard time, especially in trying to keep somewhere in sight. Finally, I look in the mirror and say, "It can't be done." If you can survive the first 21 years of a son and watch him do a lot better than yourself, then you can really enjoy it.

PRAYER

You cannot pray the Lord's Prayer,
    And even once say *I*.
You cannot pray the Lord's Prayer,
    And even once say *My*.
You cannot pray the Lord's Prayer,
    And not include another.
You cannot ask for daily bread,
    For others are included
    In each and every plea,
And from the very beginning,
    The Lord's Prayer never once says, *Me*.

(Author Unknown)

When an argument flares up, the wise man quenches it by silence. *(Ralph Waldo Emerson)*

* * *

Those who bring sunshine to others cannot keep it from themselves. *(James Barrey)*

* * *

Keep your face to the sunshine and all shadows will fall behind. *(Helen Keller)*

* * *

The surest steps toward happiness are the church steps. *(Paul Holdcraft)*

* * *

Not until we see Him in the shadow of the cross, with all its significance, do we really begin to comprehend the depth of His love!

* * *

Stop worrying about what Junior will do when he grows up. Better see what he's up to now. *(Scott Himstead)*

* * *

Give a man charity and he will come back for more; give a man help and he will help himself. *(Sunshine Magazine)*

* * *

The highest reward a man can receive for his toil is not what he gets for it but what he becomes by it. *(Church Bulletin)*

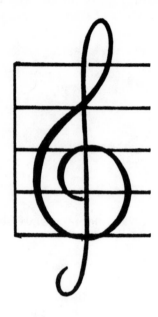

HOW HYMNS ARE BORN

Something happened to stir and inspire every writer whoever penned a hymn. We worship by singing these great church hymns and hurry by without ever realizing how they were born.

Joseph Scriven was a graduate of Trinity College, Dublin, Ireland. He early migrated to Canada and settled at Port Hope, midway on the northern shore of Lake Ontario.

Dr. Ira Sankey, the Gospel singer with Dwight L. Moody, told how a neighbor, sitting up with Scriven during a severe illness, found the manuscript of this hymn written after the death of his sweetheart, who was drowned the night before they were to be married. Joe Scriven did not say, "Why did God do this to me?" but went out in the woods all alone and wrote "What a Friend We Have in Jesus."

214

This hymn has been sung all over the English-speaking world. It may not be the best of poetry but it has a tremendous lesson of trusting in God. What Joe is doing in this hymn is pouring out his heart after his sweetheart's death, in loneliness to God. His sadness drove him to "The Rock That Is Higher Than I." Someone asked him about this hymn and he said, "The Lord and I Did It Between Us."

An unlearned person can understand this hymn and a saint can be lifted by it. It has been such a comfort to thousands of folks. After all, Christ is our best friend.

> What a friend we have in Jesus,
>   All our sins and griefs to bear!
> What a privilege to carry
>   Everything to God in prayer!
> O what peace we often forfeit,
>   O what needless pain we bear,
> All because we do not carry
>   Everything to God in prayer!

Never suffer a thought to be harbored in your mind which you would not avow openly. When tempted to do anything in secret, ask yourself if you would do it in public. If you would not, be sure it is wrong. *(Thomas Jefferson)*

JUST AS I AM

When Charlotte Elliot's parents gave a debut for her 18th birthday party over 200 guests were invited.

After the festivities, dances and dinner, the old gray-haired minister, who had been the family clergical leader for 25 years, seemed to want to give a benediction on the gathering of people. He called the people to attention and gave a gracious benedictory type of prayer. Then, for some reason, he tried to talk, privately, to Charlotte, about serious issues in her life ahead. But Charlotte, "young and restless," just did not have time for all that, at the moment. She lost her poise, talked back to him and dashed upstairs.

She did not return. The father and mother, through their evident embarrassment and clouded eyes, said "goodnight" to all of the guests.

Charlotte did not sleep. She tossed all night. She knew why the minister had struck such a sensitive chord in her being. She knew that she had become a young woman now and she had to make a choice that had been disturbing her for years.

By dawn she had a decision. She climbed out of her bed and wrote,

> Just as I am, without one plea,
> But that Thy blood was shed for me,
> And that Thou bidst me come to Thee,
> O, Lamb of God, I come, I come!
>
> Just as I am Thou wilt receive,
> Wilt welcome, pardon, cleanse, relieve;
> Because Thy promise I believe,
> O, Lamb of God, I come, I come!

216

These words of Charlotte's have helped people. Moody, Sankey and Billy Graham have used it. Many leaders who challenge folk to walk the Christian way use it.

"Him that cometh to Me, I will in no wise cast out."

When I was a lad taking care of a doctor's horses in order to go to high school, the doctor would sometimes go around the house singing:

> Today is the day they give babies away
>> With half a pound of tea.
> You open the lid and out pops a kid
>> With a written guarantee.
> Some are black and some are white
>> And some are just as cute, as cute can be.
> Oh! Today is the day they give babies away
>> With half a pound of tea.

> *(Older Than I and Unknown)*

I WILL SING OF MY REDEEMER

My mother was raised in Ohio, not far from the scene of the following wreck and, as a boy, she was now and then telling me this story.

As a young man, Philip Bliss conducted old-fashioned singing schools. With him you always saw an antique, "old-fangled" organ that he transported with him. For him, writing came naturally. Often he composed both the lyric and the musical score.

D. L. Moody, the great evangelist of that day, persuaded him to give up his travelling job, join the Christian Crusades of the Moody campaign, and help men decide for Christ.

About a dozen years before I was born, Philip Bliss was on his way to lead the inspirational music in D. L. Moody's Tabernacle. As the train which he was on approached Ashtabula, Ohio, a railroad bridge collapsed. A serious train wreck with many injuries was the result.

As a little boy, my mother often told me the story of how Mr. Bliss, himself, miraculously escaped injury. He discovered that his wife was not with him. Without hesitating he returned to the wrecked, burning cars to attempt to find his wife and save her. Both of them burned together. Their charred bodies were found side by side.

Mr. Bliss had baggage in the baggage car which was rescued. In the luggage, inspectors found this hymn that he had just written and dated.

> I will sing of my Redeemer
> And His wondrous love to me;
> On the cruel cross He suffered,
> From the curse to set ME free.

Sing, oh sing, of my Redeemer,
With His blood He purchased me,
On the cross He sealed my pardon
Paid the debt, and made me free.

"I Will Sing of My Redeemer" was his greatest contribution to the field of sacred music. As it did in the days of early evangelical song leaders, the words stirred the hearts of people. It does so yet . . . today.

As a boy in school I had a rough time remembering how to spell *Geography* until someone told me to memorize this sentence, then use the first letter of each word: *George Eason's old Grandfather rode a pig home yesterday.* That did the trick . . . . and still does!

THE OLD RUGGED CROSS

George Bennard's father died when he was only a boy of 16. The teenage boy was left with a mother and four sisters to care for. His long dreamed-of education for the ministry was postponed for many years.

His difficult years were those in which he assumed the responsibility of caring for his family. The struggle and hard work demanded of him a discipline which repaid him in later life.

After his marriage he and his wife became members and, later, officers of the Salvation Army. Years later he became a minister in the Methodist Church.

The crucifixion of Christ made an indelible impression on his mind. He based much of his ministry on the Cross and the Christ of the Cross. George Bennard became a well-known evangelistic preacher. Everywhere he went he challenged men, in all walks of life, to leave whatever it was they were doing that was wrong and walk in the right direction, choosing to do that which was right.

In 1911, George Bennard sat down with my good wife and I for an evening meal. Just two years later he penned what is often considered one of, if not, the, great American hymn entitled, The Old Rugged Cross.

He was rumored to have been at a meeting in Pokagon, between Dowagiac and Niles, Michigan, when he finished writing the words to The Old Rugged Cross. It was sung for the very first time in that parsonage home and then in the church.

Any hymnal that carries this great sacred song attributes both the words and music to George Bennard.

On a hill far away stood an old rugged cross,
The emblem of suffering and shame;
And I love that old cross where the dearest and best
For a world of lost sinners was slain.

So I'll cherish the old rugged cross
'Til my trophies at last I lay down;
I will cling to the old rugged cross,
And exchange it some day for a crown.

Friend wife seldom went with me on my missionary travels in the Upper Peninsula. First, the going was fast and rough at times. Secondly, she stayed home to raise the children and settle the questionables of which I am sure, Alvin caused many.

THERE IS A FOUNTAIN
FILLED WITH BLOOD

William Cowper was so, oh, so discouraged with himself and his life, that he felt it was useless to go on. In a moment of deep depression when he just could not reason with himself he made a decision. He would call a "cabbie." The man could drive him to the River Thames, in southern England. He would just drown himself in this swiftly-flowing water.

The "cabbie" kept driving around and around because the fog was so dense that he hardly knew how to find the River Thames. He had no visibility. Finally Cowper said to him, "Do you know where you are, cabbie?"

"No," replied the cabbie. "I guess we are lost."

"Pull right up here to the curb," said Cowper. "I'll go into this house and see where we are."

Unbelievable as it may seem, he walked directly up to his own door. He shuffled his way through the fog back to the cab to pay the driver. He returned to his house, sat down and wrote:

> There is a fountain filled with blood
>   Drawn from Emmanuel's veins;
> And, sinners plunged beneath that floor,
>   Lose all their guilt and stain.
>
> The dying thief rejoiced to see
>   That fountain in his day;
> And there may I, tho' vile as he,
>   Wash all my sins away.

. . . This is an eternal fountain from which the water ever flows.

LOVE DIVINE

This is truly a hymn of the Christian way, written by Charles Wesley (the poet of Methodism), the greatest hymnologist of all time. This is but one of his 6000 hymns. To me, this hymn is in every verse a prayer. A prayer that echoes great religious freedom and power.

"Joy of heaven to earth come down." This is the incarnation. "For God so loved." It tells us that Christ is pure, unbounded love.

When I was a boy I went for four succeeding nights to hear Gypsy Smith preach. Each evening he announced that tomorrow night he would preach on John 3:16. I could only attend four nights but he actually preached for six weeks and never changed his text. This he could do because the Christian plan is wrapped up in this verse, "For God so loved the world that he gave his only begotten Son, that whosoever believeth in him should not perish, but have everlasting life."

Wesley put this in verse, then came the music, "Changed from glory unto glory." In other words, we grow in grace. This is a great hymn that every congregation loves to sing.

> Love Divine all love excelling,
>   Joy of heav'n to earth come down:
> Fix in us Thy humble dwelling,
>   All Thy faithful mercies crown:
> Jesus, Thou art all compassion,
>   Pure, unbounded love Thou art:
> Visit us with Thy salvation;
>   Enter every trembling heart

Finish then Thy new creation,
    Pure and spotless let us be;
Let us see Thy great salvation
    Perfectly restored in Thee:
Changed from glory into glory,
    Till in heav'n we take our place,
Till we cast our crowns before Thee,
    Lost in wonder, love and praise.

And now for whom the telephone tolls; if thou art in the tub, it tolls for thee!

Unknown

AMAZING GRACE

When he was only 11 years of age, John Newton was sailing, at sea on a ship, as a worker. On this particular ship his father was the captain. John did not like where he was, what he was doing or anything about the rough life at sea. When he saw an opportunity to desert he did so. But he was caught and returned to the same ship. Unhappy as he already was, things were made worse by his having to work for a while on a slave ship. His natural shyness and fear of people, plus his somewhat captive-worker status, led to his becoming desperately degraded and degenerated.

Whenever he could get away he read whatever he could find to read. When he was a little older he read *The Imitation of Christ*. The book changed his life. As soon as possible he left this work at sea and sailed to England. He had many plans. One of them was to hunt up a girl, Mary Calett, who had been a childhood sweetheart for a short while in happier days. (Eventually he found her and later married her.)

Returning from the trip by sea to London, England, John had a great challenge to face. He thought he had left the life at sea behind him but this particular ship ran into a giant storm which threatened to swamp the ship completely. No one on ship thought he would see land again. Like John he cried out to the Lord for help. And, help actually came. John was so overcome by this goodness and grace of God that many years later he studied for the ministry. A clergy for the church of England was where he concluded his life's work.

After a cruel, sometimes abusive, childhood John Newton was the man who gave our world the great hymn of God's grace.

Amazing grace, how sweet the sound.
    That saved a wretch like me;
I once was lost but now am found,
    Was blind but now I see.

Through many dangers, toils and snares,
    I have already come;
'Tis grace hath brought me safe thus far,
    And grace will lead me home.

To me the hymn says that we are all sinners. The "Amazing Grace" of Christ, the Saviour, is what makes us feel at home and eventually leads us "Home."

When God measures a man, He puts a tape around his heart instead of his head.

Sunshine Magazine

ABIDE WITH ME

Life was not easy for Henry Lyte. For many years of his lifetime he knew poverty and illness. Eventually he did manage to take "orders" and was appointed to a small seashore parish. He spent 24 years in this one parish. This in itself is a remarkable feat.

Henry Lyte was fond, very fond, of children. His churches always had one of the very best Sunday Schools to be found (something over 600 children) and from this little fishing parish he gave to the world over 100 hymns.

Once Henry Lyte was called to the bedside of a dying man. The man kept repeating, "Abide with me. Abide with me." From this, this one touching incident, he gathered the initial inspiration to write one of the world's great hymns. He left the words unused for many years. After much time had passed he began to lose his constant battle with illness. Tuberculosis was sapping his final strength and he knew it. He went down by the sea, sat on a big rock and rewrote this hymn. Later it was used at the wedding of one of the Queens of England.

The following morning, after completing the words exactly as he wanted them for the final time, he left on a journey. He was never to return. He had chosen to go to the Alps, to a land of sunshine. After a long physical fight and great devotion to his task of serving the Lord, he wanted to leave looking up at the mountains.

When I served the Norway Methodist Church in the Upper Peninsula of Michigan, I had in my congregation a young lady teacher by the name of O'Haren, whom I have never quite forgotten. She could whistle as no one I have ever met before or since. Often the people would request that she put on a 30-minute program of whistling Christian hymns—nothing else. Invariably she finished her program with "Abide With Me" as a benediction.

Abide with me fast falls the eventide;
The darkness deepens; Lord, with me abide!
When other helpers fail and comforts flee,
Help of the helpless, O, abide with me.

If today or tomorrow it would be your privilege to stand beside the marker in the cemetery where Henry Lyte has been laid to rest you would read this inscription:

"Heaven's morning breaks, and earth's vain shadows flee,
In life, in death, O Lord, abide with me."

Husband: I'm wearing my golf socks today.
Wife: What golf socks?
Husband: You know, the ones with eighteen holes in them.

(Central Church Bulletin)

TRUST AND OBEY

One evening a man, Daniel Towner, was leading the music for D. L. Moody's campaign. This Mr. Towner happened to hear a young man say, "I'm not quite sure about being a Christian but anyway I am going to trust and obey."

Mr. Towner gave these few, simple words to a Presbyterian minister, a man by the name of John Sammis. He developed the idea into a beautiful hymn.

> When we walk with the Lord
> In the light of His word,
> What a glory He sheds on our way.
> While we do His good will,
> He abides with us still,
> And with all who will trust and
> obey.
>
> Trust and obey,
> For, there's no other way
> To be happy in Jesus,
> But to trust and obey.

When I was serving a church in Traverse City, Michigan, we were badly in need of some new song books for the Sunday School. A young woman by the name of Ruth Wysong said to me one day, "I will buy 100 new hymn books for the church school. You can select the book—just as long as it has Trust and Obey in it."

"Trust and Obey." Long, oh, long ago I learned that I can trust God better than I can trust Alvin.

BLESSED ASSURANCE

I believe that Joseph Knapp founded the Metropolitan Life Insurance Company. His good wife, Phoebe, was an accomplished singer and a composer of music. In time she became known as a creator of excellent melodies. She would often compose the music, then find someone else to write the lyric.

One of Phoebe Knapp's best friends was Fanny Crosby, who was blinded early in life. Fanny had a creative mind and was gifted in music. One day Phoebe Knapp wrote a tune which she then played for Fanny Crosby. She turned to her and asked, "What words would go with it?" The blind Fanny, who wrote between 6,000 and 7,000 hymns, replied with these words:

> Blessed Assurance Jesus is mine:
> O, what a foretaste of glory divine,
> Heir of Salvation purchased of God;
> Born of His Spirit, washed in His blood.
>
> This is my story, this is my song;
> Praising my Saviour all the day long;
> This is my story, this is my song
> Praising my Saviour all the day long.

To me these words are a sort of a "Foretaste of glory." They express confidence and happiness in the Christian Way.

Fanny Crosby and Phoebe Knapp collaborated many times, combining their musical talents. One of their joint efforts is entitled, "Open the Gates of the Temple." This hymn is often used at Easter time or at church dedications.

So often through my ministry when the choir failed to have a special number I would say, "Let's all play choir and sing Blessed Assurance."

230

IT IS WELL WITH MY SOUL

About two years after the great Chicago fire in which Horatio Stafford lost most of his earthly belongings his wife wanted to return to Europe with the family of four children. The rapid rebuilding of Chicago, after the fire, demanded Horatio's time and money. Although his responsibilities detained him, he encouraged his wife to finally take the children and sail for the continent.

The luxury ship on which the family sailed was rammed by an English liner. Although many of the people were saved, 200 voyagers were lost. Numbered among those missing were the four Stafford children.

Mrs. Stafford did what she had to do. She continued on for nine desolate days—entirely alone. When she finally landed with the passengers who had been saved she sent this cablegram to her husband, back home in Chicago:

"SAVED ALONE."

Realizing what his wife had gone through he booked passage as soon as possible. Nothing in Chicago mattered now. He would join his bereaved wife.

On the trip across the water the captain said to Mr. Stafford, "We are now passing almost directly over the place where your four children were drowned."

This seemed to be the final bend in Mr. Stafford's life-long search for peace. Touched by the loss of the great fire and left brokenhearted by the loss of his four children, Mr. Stafford went to his stateroom and wrote:

> When peace like a river attendeth my way,
> When sorrows like sea billows roll,
> Whatever my lot, Thou hast taught me to say,
> It is well, it is well, with my soul.

Philip Bliss, who wrote the music to this comforting hymn of resignation, is the same man who died, with his wife, in a train wreck near Ashtabula, Ohio. How wonderful that both the lyric and score were composed by a man who could say, "It is well, with my soul."

I still recall that as a young minister many, many years ago my very first funeral was that of a 12-year-old girl. She had been drowned in the Chippewa River, west of Midland, Michigan. The family requested that at her funeral service everyone sing, "It is well, it is well, with my soul."

When death the great reconciler has come, it is never our tenderness that we repent but our severity.
(George Elliot)

LET THE LOWER LIGHTS BE BURNING

"Brightly Beams Our Father's Mercy" is another title sometimes substituted for this hymn. I believe that the original title does a finer job of saying what the author, Phillip Bliss, wanted said. He is the same man who also composed the hymn, "I Will Sing of My Redeemer."

Reverend Thomas Stubbs was the circuit preacher when I was courting my wife, Iva Lisk, in 1909-1910. One day in his sermon he told the following story, in these words: "In my younger days I was a sailor on the Great Lakes. One night in a terrific storm we had a most difficult time making the Cleveland harbor. This experience of mine reminded me of a pilot who had a similar experience in a dangerous storm. He, too, was trying to make the same harbor.

Lake Erie was rough that night, very rough. Not a single star was to be seen. The captain said to the pilot, "Where are the 'lower lights'?" . . . "Gone out," was the pilot's reply. "Can you make the harbor?" the captain asked. "We *must,* or we are lost," the pilot replied. Then he struggled against great odds in the blinding gale; but, he missed the channel. The ship and many lives were lost because, "The Lower Lights Were Not Burning."

The author of this hymn, Phillip Bliss, wrote both the words and the music. He and his wife also died tragically in a fire immediately following a train wreck. It was known at the time as the Ashtabula train wreck.

The last verse of the hymn reminds me of my boyhood days. One of the most simple tasks my mother gave to me to accomplish was that of trimming off the burned portion of the wicks, in all the lamps and lanterns. (If you did this the lamps would not smoke up the glass chimneys the following night.) It was a daily task if you wanted good bright lights.

233

As I remember Tom Stubbs' story, the lighthouse was burning; but, the lower harbor lights were out. *This was why the pilot lost his ship and many lives!*

The evangelist, Gypsy Smith, used this hymn when I was a lad. Later, Billy Sunday also used it, almost every night, in his world famous campaigns.

> Brightly beams our Father's mercy
> From His lighthouse evermore.
> But to us He gives the keeping
> Of the lights, along the shore.
>
> Dark the night of sin has settled,
> Loud the angry billows roar;
> Eager eyes are watching, longing,
> For the lights along the shore.
>
> Trim your feeble lamp, my brother;
> Some poor sailor tempest-tossed.
> Trying now to make the harbor,
> In the darkness, may be lost.
>
> REFRAIN
> Let the lower lights be burning!
> Send a gleam across the wave!
> Some poor fainting, struggling seaman
> You may rescue, you may save.

We can't all be lighthouses; but, each one of us can, at least, be a *lower light*.

Learn from the mistakes of others. You can't live long enough to make them all yourself. *(Pulpit Digest)*

234

HOLY, HOLY, HOLY

Reginald Heber was born in England, born into a family of great wealth. Somehow the money was just there. It meant little to him. Both in England and, on the other side of the world, in India, he gave his life to God. His greatest position was that of Bishop of Calcutta, India, for the Anglican Church.

Though being a bishop may have been his position, it was not his power but his passion that ruled him. All through his life and his ministries, even in his administrative positions, he still tried to improve the hymn singing of the church he loved.

Because of his abiding, consuming love of sacred music he was able to give to the church and to the Christian world this great hymn, based on the 4th chapter of Revelations.

Holy, Holy, Holy! Lord God Almighty!
　　Early in the morning, our song shall rise to Thee;
Holy, Holy, Holy! Merciful and Mighty!
　　God in three persons, blessed Trinity!

Holy, Holy, Holy! All the saints adore Thee,
　　Casting down their golden crowns
　　around the glassy sea;
Cherubim and seraphim falling down before Thee,
　　Which wert and art, and evermore shall be.

Who else could have penned to music the doctrine of the Trinity and the story of the angels worshipping God in His own heaven?

IN THE GARDEN

In my early ministry I attended the Billy Sunday Campaigns and he used this hymn a great deal.

So many people, even musicians, have said to me, "This hymn, 'I Come to the Garden Alone,' doesn't seem to have too much meaning to it." Austin Miles, who wrote this hymn, was really writing about the Easter morning. Can't you see Mary in the sepulchre garden and hear her saying, "Raboni"—which means "Master." Mary came early, very early, on an Easter morning, "While the dew was still on the roses." "He speaks and the sound of His voice . . . " Jesus said, "Mary." She recognized her Lord. Once you stop to realize where this garden was located, this hymn has an overwhelming meaning.

Jesus said, "Touch Me not; for I am not yet ascended to my Father: but go to my brethren and say unto them, I ascend unto my Father; and your Father; and to my God and to your God."

I come to the garden alone,
    While the dew is still on the roses;
And the voice I hear, falling on my ear,
    The Son of God discloses.

And He walks with me, and He talks with me,
    And He tells me I am His own,
And the joy we share as we tarry there,
    None other has ever known.

236

BLEST BE THE TIE

Long ago a Reverend John Fawcett was the minister in Wainsgate, a small town near London, England. He had served there successfully for over six years when he received a call to follow a highly competent man into a large London city church. The congregation of his church and all of the people of the small town of Wainsgate were most reluctant to think of his leaving them. But, they could not honestly make any attempt to keep him from moving up into a well-known church pulpit. They even helped the pastor and his wife with the final packing and cleaning of the manse.

When the moving day arrived and all had been packed into the huge wagons, John Fawcett discovered his faithful wife was in a most despondent mood. Getting her off away from the people he questioned her, "What's wrong with you, wife?" She answered, "I am just not at all certain that we are doing the right thing in leaving Wainsgate for the big church in London."

After a few moments of quietness John said, "I feel exactly the same way."

The Reverend John Fawcett sat down and wrote a letter of resignation. He advised the Pastoral Relations Committee and the congregation of the prominent London church of their joint decision to stay in Wainsgate.

The people of the little town unloaded and unpacked with much more zeal. It was then, when he saw how the people loved them and the Lord, that John Fawcett penned these beautiful words:

> Blest be the tie that binds,
> Our hearts in the Christian love;
> The fellowship of kindred minds,
> Is like to that above.

When we asunder part,
It gives us inward pain;
But we shall still be joined in heart,
And hope to meet again.

This great hymn asking for His blessing on any closing session was written by a man who for 51 years, along with his wife, served the fellowship of "kindred minds" in Wainsgate, England.

My wife and I and our children like to believe that God dwells in our house, so we feel it is only proper that we should return the courtesy of visiting Him in His house. *(Sam Levensen)*

CHURCH WINDOWS

As a young preacher, my second District Superintendent, Dr. Charles Baldwin, after whom Baldwin Hall at Albion College is named, said to me, "Brother Doten, a sermon without illustrations is like a house without windows." This analogy was pertinent and powerful. I never forgot it.

Ofttimes folks said that I told too many stories. But what about the parables of Jesus? To me this was an outstanding facet of Christ's ministry. In my many years as a minister, the following illustrations are a few of the many that I used to help folks remember the truth. These are stories of courage and inspiration that challenged men to walk the Christian Way.

These church windows were gleaned by listening to Billy Sunday preach and taking notes as fast as I could. (Billy Sunday was a baseball player who became the world's greatest evangelist preceding Billy Graham.)

Many of these illustrations came from listening to men like Arthur Stalker, 21 years minister at Ann Arbor. Others were discovered in the *Sunday School Times* (the greatest study help I have ever known).

Illustrations reprinted from the *Sunday School Times* are used by permission.

TYPEWRITER

A young man graduated from Leland Stanford University's School of Engineering. At the time of his graduation, Louis Jensen of San Francisco had the name of being the world's outstanding mining engineer. The young engineer decided that Jensen would be a good man to go and see, with the hope of getting into business with him one day.

It was just before noon on a Friday when he was ushered into Louis Jensen's office. Mr. Jensen told him that he already had five engineers; but, in actuality, because of the hard times, he only needed one. He had kept the others in his service because of their families. Then he said, "What I do need now, and badly, is someone who can run a typewriter."

The young engineer excused himself. He showed up again the following Tuesday morning. Louis Jensen said, "I am surprised to see you back. If you can type, what in the world was so important to you that you did not go to work last Friday, instead of waiting until Tuesday?"

The young man answered, "Mr. Jensen, I went out last Friday and rented a typewriter. Since then I have learned to run it."

Mr. Jensen said, "I think you'll do. I did not ask your name last Friday. What is it?" The young man answered, "Herbert Hoover."

I am wondering just how badly we want God anyway. How much are we willing to put into it to seek Him? How much do we want Him to control our lives? Are we willing to put enough into it to say, with the poet writer, James Small:

240

I've found a friend O such a friend!
He loved me ere I knew Him.
He drew me with the cords of love
And thus He bound me to Him.
And round my heart still closely twine
Those ties which naught can sever,
For, I am His and He is mine,
Forever and forever.

NOONTIDE MUSIC

I think of John Wanamaker who became Postmaster General. Long before that he had become America's foremost merchant of his day, with great stores in New York and Philadelphia. He had pipe organs installed in each of these stores. And even if a clerk were waiting on you and had a package half-wrapped, at 11:45 a.m. everything stopped as the organ pealed out the great hymns of the Christian church. For 15 minutes the aisles would be packed. At exactly 12:00 noon the organ stopped, the clerk finished wrapping your package and gave you your change!

Someone once asked John Wanamaker, "What in your life of leadership in business was the greatest purchase you ever made?" His answer was, "A little red colored New Testament that I bought for $1.25 when I was a 14-year-old canal boy on the Erie Canal. On this book I built my life and my business."

If you think one individual can't make a difference in the world, remember what one cigar can do in a nine-room house! *(Bill Vaughn)*

THE DOCTOR AND THE LITTLE BOY

A young doctor became a very successful surgeon. In spite of this he always had time for a Sunday school class that averaged about 20 boys. Life, however, became very full. He forgot the church and his class of boys.

One day as this doctor was ready to operate on a little fellow he said, "Now, lie down, Sonny, and the anesthetist will put you to sleep."

"Just a minute," said the boy. "I'm not quite ready, doctor." He hopped off the table and onto his knees. He placed his two little hands together and said:

> "Now I lay me down to sleep
> I pray the Lord my soul to keep.
> If I should die before I wake,
> I pray the Lord my soul to take.
> This I ask for Jesus' sake. Amen."

"Now, I'm ready, doctor." But the doctor was not quite ready. He went into his office, lay his head in his hands, on his desk and said, "O Lord, I've forgotten my boys and I've forgotten the church. Help me save the life of this little fellow and I'll come back." The doctor kept his word, his promise to God. The last we knew of him he had 44 boys in his Sunday school class.

Have we kept our promise to Him?

There is so much good in the worst of us, and so much bad in the best of us, that we need law and religion for all of us. *(Louis Nizer)*

CALLING

It is related by one familiar with oriental shepherds, that the flock is often called by the notes of a little flute-like instrument. A number of flocks may be feeding together, but when the shepherd puts his flute to his lips and gives his own peculiar note, his own sheep immediately leave the company and follow him.

Another shepherd will give his evening call so much like the other that a stranger can observe no difference. But the sheep know the difference. Just the ones that belong to the master follow him, and no other. "My sheep hear my voice, and I know them and they follow me."

The missionary who related these facts, took the instrument and endeavored to imitate the call. But the sheep only raised their heads in alarm, looking this way and that, as if about to flee. "A stranger will they not follow, for they know not the voice of strangers."

How precious the thought that Christ knows all his sheep by name, and all their peculiarities. He is always ready to help us over the rough places if we only look up trustingly to Him.

"The sheep hear his voice; and he calleth his own sheep by name, and leadeth them out."

I have been driven many times to my knees by the overwhelming conviction that I had nowhere else to go. *(Abraham Lincoln)*

TWO CHOICES

We all know the story of David Livingstone, a Scottish youth who studied theology and medicine, then gave his life to opening up the continent of Africa.

A ragged, "downright" bum was walking along in the funeral procession for David Livingstone. Someone rebuked him for crowding in, dressed as frightfully poorly as he was. Do you know what the man said? This is it.

"I have a right to be here. David Livingstone and I went to Sunday school together. He decided *for* Christ and I decided against Him."

Have you decided?

BEAUTIFUL HANDS

Years ago I read a story of a boy who came in from his play one day and suddenly noticed his mother's gnarled hands.

"Mother," he said. "You have such terrible looking hands."

"Run back to your play," replied his mother. "When your friends have gone and we are alone I will tell you about my hands."

Later he eagerly said, "Now, mama, they are gone. Tell me about your hands."

His mother held him on her lap and told him this story.

"This is true, sonny. When you were a little fellow, creeping on the floor, you came too close to the fireplace. Your little dress caught fire. Mother rubbed the fire all out. That is what is the matter with my hands."

This little boy, with more gratitude than many of us have or show, took his mother's hands in his tiny fingers and said,

"Mother, they are the most beautiful hands in all the world."

The mother must have been happier, more contented than she had been in a long time. She had waited for the right moment to share her story with her son.

I do not know of anything in all this world that can make you quite as happy or at peace as helping someone else and believing in it—knowing it is worthwhile!

HARD KNOT

About 20 years ago, my preacher son, Donn, tied a slipknot for a very interesting young couple. After many years of married life, they were divorced, and each went his or her own way on life's journey.

This singular journey lasted about 11 months. Theirs was a mutual decision that this was not the better arrangement. They secured a second marriage license. This time around they came to Papa Doten. So this time we married them in Faith Chapel at Hill Top Manor, and we pulled a hardknot.

This is a concrete example of love triumphing over pride and the opinions of others. They found the understanding needed to continue caring. They *cared less* what the world thought about it.

THANKSGIVING

Six years before I was born, a visitor to Northern Michigan, in 1882, tells of being led by his host to the mouth of the famous Calumet and Hecla Copper Mine a little before five o'clock in the afternoon. "Stand here and listen," said his friend. There was silence for a moment and then, coming from the earth behind their feet, faint sounds were heard. They grew stronger and more distinct as they waited, seeming like the weird melodies played by the wind on telegraph wires. Nearer and nearer they came, mingled with the creaking of machinery, and resolving themselves at last into the familiar notes of "Nearer My God to Thee."

The cage reached the top of the shaft, and the day shift of Welsh miners, who had been singing their way up from a depth of hundreds of feet, stepped out and, baring their heads, joined in, "Praise God from Whom All Blessings Flow," and then quietly turned homeward. "They do this every night when their work is done," said the host. "It is their expression of praise and thanksgiving."

"And one of them when he saw that he was healed, turned back, and with a loud voice glorified God."

A French surgeon of the 1600s had a sign which read: *I dressed the wound and God healed it.*

These numbers are mine or stories 60 years old.

1

NED SPENCER

Every age has its collegiate athletes. Today we hear about "Magic" Johnson, of Michigan State University and Larry Byrd of Indiana State University. Long years ago a name that many knew was Ned Spencer. He was an outstandingly strong athlete of Northwestern University, Evanston, Illinois.

One day when Ned was home on break from school, he was alarmed to hear that a ship, the *Lady Elgin* (if my memory serves me right . . .) was wrecked not too terribly far from their shoreline.

"Quickly," he said, without hesitating. "Get me a small but very strong rope, at the hardware. Meet me at the shore."

With the help of others he tied this rope tightly about his waist. Then he said to the people of his hometown, "I will swim out and save someone and you folks pull me back." And he did just that. It worked so well that 28 times they pulled him back with one of the passengers or one of the crew of the boat. He was beyond the point of exhaustion when he quit. For, he did not quit until every last man was off that boat.

The story itself is almost unbelievable; but, wait! There is something even more incredible. Ned Spencer spent the rest of his life in a wheelchair *and not one person* ever sent him a card or a flower.

If we have any flowers to give, let's give them now!

2

SAWMILL

When I was a boy I worked in a sawmill. There were three very important jobs in that mill. The fireman who kept up steam to give the mill power, the sawyer who controlled the levers that delivered the power to the big circular saw that made lumber, planks or 2 x 4s. Then there was the setter, the one who rode the moving carriage and kept his balance to keep from falling on the big whirling saw as the carriage returned in a rush to take another board or plank off the log. I was a small boy but quick and had good balancing power so I drew this job. You learned to read sawyers signals by the signs he made with his fingers but it was a very dangerous job.

The sawyer was the key man. He was paid $1.50 a day, the fireman $1.00 and as a mere lad of 12 years I was that setter and received 75 cents a day. All other helpers about the mill were paid 50 cents a day and all these men would like to have eaten me for a sandwich because I received 75 cents.

If you have ever been around a mill you know that the boiler has a glass tube that shows you how much water is in the boiler. If you let the water get too high you had almost no room for steam to make power, if you let the water get too low the boiler would blow and the explosion meant death. The trick was to carry just enough water in the boiler to give power.

I am sure the gauge on our living is like the love we show to our brother, our neighbors and our fellow man. To me this becomes the measure of our love for God.

"Thou shalt love the Lord thy God with all thy heart,
and with all thy soul, and with all thy mind.
This is the first and great commandment.
And the second is like unto it. Thou shalt
love thy neighbor as thyself."

These two added commandments are not, by any
means, an easy command.

I returned from the lumber camps and the Indians only
to receive a ticket to despair. In the early morning I complained that something was biting me. I turned back the
covers and there was a gray-backed louse. Friend wife was
startled and indignant, and she abruptly replied, "Alvin
Doten, I will never sleep with you again as long as I live."
But she repented.

THE LONGEST DAY

Time! A universal commodity that we are unsure of, surrounds us, limits us, controls us and even changes us.

Time is, of course, a variable. A state or local government each has the legal power to adopt at its discretion, a new time and give it a name all its own, perhaps Daylight Savings Time.

According to the Encyclopedia International, Volume No. 5, Eastern Daylight Time was established to save lighting expenses during both World War I and World War II.

Time—how arbitrary it is. The two natural cycles on which time measurements are based are the *year* and the *day*. Yet, while time zones are based on the natural event of the sun crossing the Meridian, the dates are arbitrary.

Did you ever ask yourself this question: "Where will the longest day be found?" Obviously this answer would depend considerably on where you are at the time.

"In New York state the longest day would be 15 hours; in Montreal, Canada, 16 hours; in London, England, 16½ hours; in Stockholm, Sweden, Baltic Sea Port, 18½ hours; in the Faroe Islands, 22 hours; in Wardbury, Norway, 2 months; and in Spitzbergen, the Norwegian Sea, it would be 3½ months . . . "

Yes, "Time waits for no man." To determine the sunrise and the sunset, you need to know the longitude and the latitude at a given place.

The longitude of your life and the latitude, or breadth, are determined by the rising sun, the Son of God!

In the New Jerusalem, all who *"believe* in the Lord Jesus Christ," will find the longest day. As the Good Book says, "There shall be no night there."

5
STICK-TO-IT-IVENESS

I often feel that the good things we have are ours because of some other person's stick-to-it-iveness.

George Washington, the Father of our country, surely possessed it. Guisseppe Garibaldi, the Italian reformer, surely had it. I can see him now drawing a line on the ground in front of his discouraged troops. I can hear him saying, "On that side of the line lies home and your sweethearts; but on this side lies a free Italy. Who dares to cross the line and come with me?" And every man crossed that line.

God gave Abraham Lincoln an old pine knot which he burned on a shovel by which to read. With his spirit and knowledge he eventually struck the shackles from the slaves. It cost him his life. He chose the right instead of the wrong. This demands real courage. Wilfred Grenfell possessed the same spirit of persistence in his ministry to Labrador. There probably are not enough letters in the dictionary to spell the courage exemplified by this man.

Albert Schweitzer, son of a clergyman and his wife, daughter of another clergyman, were a great team. Albert Schweitzer was a doctor, a theologian, preacher, lecturer, missionary, musician, builder and organizer. Founding the hospital at Lambarene, Africa, was only one accomplishment. His contribution made him the leading citizen of his generation. His is a tremendous example of devotion and stick-to-it-iveness.

John Rowlands was raised in a workhouse in England. At 15, he ran away and became a cabin boy on a vessel bound for New Orleans. Henry Stanley adopted him. He named him Henry Morton Stanley. He first served in the Civil War and went from the Confederate side to the Union troops before it was all over.

Stanley eventually became a correspondent for the *New York Herald*. This newspaper sent him on a special assignment to Africa to look for Livingstone. (No one had heard a word about him in two years' time.) Stanley said, "We did not think of the hundreds of miles of forest we travelled, of the jungles and thickets, the salt plains, the blistering feet or the hot sun. We surmounted our difficulties and we found Livingstone. He was in a little town called Ujiji.

Stanley's was an outstanding example of courage and stick-to-it-iveness. His determination lasted for 11 long months after he had reached Africa. At my years I cannot quote Stanley exactly; but what he said was something like this: "I was a correspondent looking for news. I had little thought of religion. After we found Livingstone and watched him, something happened to me. I saw him reading his Bible, in prayer, helping others. I was utterly amazed. I watched him for months. He never changed. He lived for others . . . We tried to bring him back to England, but he stayed with his people who needed him in Africa. (One day the natives found him on his knees where he had died in the act of prayer.) I finally returned to the United States but before I did so I realized that Livingstone, by his example, had made me a man of God."

When David Livingstone died the natives buried his heart in Africa. Then they made a bark coffin and carried him 1,000 miles to the coast to be shipped back to Old England where he was buried in Westminster Abbey among Kings.

Livingstone was assistant church organist at nine, grew up and not only gave himself to Africa, but also to the world. In the midst of it all Stanley found Livingstone because of his stick-to-it-iveness.

"Be of good courage and he shall strengthen thine heart."

6

BLOOD

I had some very delicate surgery in the Little Traverse Hospital in Petoskey, Michigan. In those days Harold Jane was the minister of our church in Petoskey. This brother minister gave three pints of his blood that I might live. Later when I asked him the cost of this blood he said, "Alvin, I did not sell that blood, I gave it." That was the very spirit in which Christ gave his precious blood.

> For Jesus shed His precious blood
> Rich blessings to bestow,
> Plunge now into that crimson flood
> That washes white as snow.

It is when we help someone else that we get a great joy out of life. The best things of life are not found in a bargain basement but in a closer walk with God.

I have never been amazed that there are so many good people in the world, but I have been continually amazed that I have been fortunate enough to have met so many of them. *(Orm Danford)*

WASTE PRODUCTS

Not long ago I read about the marvelous things that are made out of waste products. Someone learned to make perfume out of coal tar. The Standard Oil Company makes a multitude of merchantable articles out of by-products of crude oil—dishes, perfume, hundreds of things. Dow Chemical does the same. In fact, I believe it was at Dow Chemical that a chemist said, "We can use any kind of waste here except wasted time."

It's more amazing what God can make out of wasted men. He took Saul, a persecutor, and made of him an outstanding character, next to His own Son in the New Testament. He took John Bunyan, a tinker-man, and gave to the world *Pilgrim's Progress*. He took a mill boy and made out of him a David Livingstone. He took a ballplayer and made of him a Billy Sunday. He took Michelangelo, gave him an ugly piece of cold marble and he made of it one of the greatest pieces of art in the world.

Think of the artistry of God, who works with material far more baffling than marble—sinful, stubborn man. God makes us so worthwhile when we help Him. I am overcome by His faith in our flesh. I have seen this in every community where I have lived, and I marvel at His love.

Any fool can count the seeds in an apple, but only God can count the apples in a seed. *(Maple Leaf)*

8

A PANACEA FOR DISCOURAGEMENT

Are you discouraged? Does it ever seem to you that the bottom has actually fallen out of the world, or at least of your world?

How discouraged were the disciples back at the time of Jesus? They had actually seen this Jesus heal the sick, make the lame walk, make the blind see and even the dead to arise again. They had worked with him. They had loved him, day after day. Do you think anyone has ever been as discouraged as His disciples once were? I can't imagine any people on the face of this earth today as discouraged as they just must have been. They *believed* in Him. For such a long time, everything had gone wrong. It was inexplicable. It was unacceptable to them.

Then, something happened. I do not need to tell you that it was Easter morning. He dispelled all their discouragements.

He will dispel all your discouragements, too, *if* you will permit Him to do so.

If we trust, Christ comes to us with the lantern of God in His hands. It is the eternal light that erases discouragement.

As Lawrence Welk would say, "It's just wonderful," when you wake up from a dream where your wife is making biscuits out of flour and sawdust.

9

DEFROSTING

Every so often my good wife gets a spell of defrosting the refrigerator. She takes every last thing out of it, lets the air in, scrapes and washes the ice, lets it dry, then fills it again and it goes to work with a new beginning.

I have never served a church that did not have some folks who needed defrosting. Sometimes I guess I needed it too. Then, too, I have seen other ministers whom I am sure needed defrosting also.

It is only the love of God that can do this, for you or for me. How much more serviceable we are when we let the love of God work through us. If you would be warm-hearted let the love of Christ work in you. It will bring happiness to you and to others. (Happiness that nothing else can bring.)

"Fill with Thy Spirit, 'til all shall be
Christ only always living in me."

10

PATRICK HENRY'S WILL

I think of Patrick Henry, that fine old pioneer, and the clause he left in his will. "I have now disposed of all my property to my family and there is one thing still that I wish I could give them. That is the Christian religion. If they have that, and I have not given them one shilling, they would be rich. But if they have it not, and I give them all the world, they will yet be poor."

11

GRANDFATHER'S HERITAGE

When I was just a little "chap" about six years old, I had an experience that has stayed with me for over 85 years.

We lived in the woodlands, near Standish, Michigan. My mother received an emergency telegram from West Independence, Ohio. She was to return, immediately, to her girlhood home because her father, Mr. George Smith, was critically ill. Hurriedly she prepared herself and me for the sad journey.

I cannot recall what grandfather or mother wore; but, to this very hour, I can visualize the little white blouse, with black deer heads on it, which she chose for me to appear in.

My grandfather had been gravely ill for nearly six weeks. (In those days, transportation was tedious. No one sent for loved ones until the terminal aspects of the illness were apparent.) Thus it was, that only two days after our arrival, my grandfather, who had not had the strength to speak for nearly six weeks, revealed the pseudo strength that often appears at the end of this earthly life.

In the superficial strength of his dying moments, grandfather lifted up his arms and wrapped them around my mother.

"Amelia, my dear," he said. "It is *gold*. It is *all gold.*"

. . . And he was gone. Gone to join that great throng whose robes had been "Washed in the Blood of the Lamb."

All the books that were ever written, in my lifetime or preceding it, against the Christian religion—all the infidels who ever lived—could not then or now ever erase that memory. What my childish eyes saw, and my little ears heard.

257

12

RE-CREATION

Is there anything more wonderful, more interesting, more attractive than the transformation of something apparently worthless into something useful and beautiful?

I think of a swamp in which horses and cattle mired. Today, on that same land, they raise carloads of onions and peppermint. It may be but a waste product that is left after they make gasoline, but out of this evidently wasteful slime come dishes and perfume and hundreds of by-products.

You sit down at the table and say, "What pretty dishes," as you eat beefsteak when some parishioner kills a beef, or you eat chicken off those dishes (if you are lucky enough to have the chicken) and you say, "My, but 'twas good," but if you could see the slime from which those dishes were made, you couldn't eat at all.

From coal tar we get perfume and dye. Out of silk sweepings comes velvet. Today, sawdust can be made into pressboard. Paint brushes from pig bristles. From the glands of cattle we get much needed medication. One of the most useful gadgets in our home is a little step stool about 10 x 12 inches with a handle about two feet high. You can pick it up, take it with you and reach an article on any shelf in the home. This gimmick is made from scrap lumber and scrap linoleum. All of these are re-creation.

You go out West and look at some of those irrigated tracts of land that were all desert and you think of what the Good Book says: "And the desert shall blossom as a rose." These, too, are re-creation. Redeemed things. But redeemed men are worth so much more than perfume, dishes and plastics, that only God can measure them. "He

258

restoreth my soul." That is the way you describe redeemed men.

"Thy people, Thou hast redeemed through Thy greatness."

I lived with a doctor to get to go to High School and he was forever telling stories. One of his stories was about a cowboy who went into New York City to eat in a fashionable restaurant. He ordered a steak. When he received his order he said to the waitress, "Why, that steak is not cooked, take it back to the cook shanty and get it cooked."

The waitress said "Why, that's cooked."

And the Texas cowboy came back: "Cooked, cooked? Lassie, I have seen steers hurt worse than that and get well."

WESTMINSTER ABBEY

It is well-known that in Westminster Abbey, the home of Britain's mighty deceased, are buried people whose names mean little today. Truly great writers, men like David Livingstone and even kings are also buried there. But, many of the people who are buried there have been forgotten by the world.

At the time of the interment anyone buried in Westminster Abbey was distinguished—so famous that nothing less than burial in the "Abbey" would satisfy. Now, after a number of generations have passed, few people really remember who is buried there and why. Such a fleeting thing is fame!

The only thing that shall last forever will be *faith* in God. Faith will bring you an Easter Morning that will last forever.

I can still hear my mother singing:

> "Angels roll the rock away
> Death yield up its mighty prey.
> See the Saviour quit the tomb,
> Glory immortal, Hallelujah bloom."

The older generation thought nothing of getting up at five every morning . . . . and the younger generation doesn't think much of it either. *(Nuggets)*

14
BOOTBLACK

Two travelling men were standing by a drinking fountain cursing because they could not make it work. A little bootblack boy heard them. He hustled over and said, "Please, Misters. If you don't swear so much I'll show you how to get a drink."

Then he reached down and touched a hidden button and the fountain flowed. This little fellow knew how to touch the hidden spring on two different fountains. God can do some wonderful things, for us, if we, like the bootblack boy, keep in tune with his magic buttons.

God took a fisherman, then another, and another. They were only men, working men. With them He set up His Kingdom.

God took a tentmaker from Tarsus. With him, God carried the cross to the throne of the Caesars.

God took a Spinning Jenny in Scotland. With him, He opened up the continent of Africa.

God sent William Carey, a shoe cobbler, to India. Without him, whoever would have heard of Lucknow College?

God took Alfred Grenfell from London and made of him an Angel to Labrador. He took a boy from a log cabin in Kentucky, gave him a pine knot to read by. With him, God struck the shackles from the slaves.

God took Albert Schweitzer, born on the River Rhine. He made of him an assistant church organist, at the age of nine. He led him on to become the world's outstanding citizen of his generation.

What He can do with us only God knows. That is—*if* we let Him?

15
SKY-LARK

Merton S. Rice was Methodism's great preacher of his generation. His early ministry was in Kansas, then nine years in Duluth, and thirty years in Metropolitan's pulpit in Detroit. For many years he was chairman of the committee on episcopacy. If there were a tie vote as to where a Bishop should be assigned, he was the man who would break that tie.

I believe M. S. Rice withdrew four different quadrenniums from the balloting for the Bishopric. But who would want to be a Bishop when he could tell the Bishops where to go—Washington, Denver, New Orleans or Calcutta?

I remember Dr. Rice giving a lecture in Bay City, Michigan. When he was introduced he held up his blue ticket and asked, "How many of you paid for your ticket to get in here tonight?" Then he added, "I did! The girl at the door would not let me pass until I bought a ticket."

That night he told a story of the late Bishop William Quayle, who was known as "Methodism's Sky-Lark," because of his masterful oratory. Merton Rice, who was often nicknamed "Mike," told of Bishop Quayle when he was on a railway journey, where he was one of several men discussing matters. Finally one of the travellers, a sales representative for a commercial firm, turned to the Bishop, whose identity he did not know, and asked, "What is your kind of business? What do you deal in?" Bishop Quayle replied, "Horizons." He said he was commissioned as a representative of Christ to lift men's eyes from the immediate and near, to the distant skyline and a beckoning goal of the Kingdom. He went on to say, "Truth reveals itself when we lift our eyes."

"I will lift up mine eyes unto the hills,
unto the hills, from whence cometh my help.
My help cometh from the Lord which made
heaven and earth."

262

SAVAGE

During the early part of our life, we spent the best part of three nights each week on the sermon. Beginning at 10:00 o'clock when folks quit coming and the phone stopped ringing. Thus it was the hours between 10:00 at night and 4:00 in the morning became our real study period.

Next to the study the most important item were the folks in the hospital. You learn to spend about eight minutes with each one, finishing always with a brief prayer. Bedside ministry becomes an art. It was not uncommon to have 26-28 people in the hospital. You learn to minister to 10 of them on Monday, 10 on Tuesday and 8 on Wednesday. Come Thursday, you start the process all over again. This way you saw each patient twice a week. To me, the night study and the hospital work were savage work hours in spite of the fact that a preacher never has anything to do?

Another savage story comes to mind. It happened when I was sky-piloting in the 15 counties of the Upper Peninsula of Michigan. My district superintendent's name was Joseph Dutton and what a time we had with our names (Dutton and Doten)! Actually not we two, but the post office and other folk. We were always getting one another's mail, as well as each other's bills. Finally, I went to the postmaster and said to him, "You have 26 Andersons in the phone book. How on earth do you keep those 26 Andersons straightened out and almost daily get Dutton and Doten mixed up?" That ended the mail problem—but not the bill troubles.

One Saturday my superintendent, Joseph Dutton, said to me, "Which way will you be working next week, East or West?" I replied, "East." He then said, "Where will you be Monday night?" I replied, "Trout Lake." (Twenty-eight miles north of the Straits of Mackinac.) It was then

Joe said, "We both have passes on the railroad, so meet me in Ferguson's Hardware in the Soo at 11:00 o'clock Tuesday morning."

Joe Dutton had an engineer brother who built railroads for the Canadian Pacific in British Columbia. When this engineer brother died, he left his preacher brother, Joe, as administrator of his estate. I believe that Joe made five trips from Marquette to Vancouver to carry out his brother's request. I am not certain as to how many brothers and sisters Joe had, but I believe each one inherited $60,000.00.

I will never forget that, when Joe met me that Tuesday morning in the Ferguson's Hardware, he said to me, "The first money I spend out of my $60,000.00 will be to buy you a gun. That is why we are here." After an hour and a half of examination we decided on a 303 Savage.

After we had decided on the Savage and some ammunition, this superintendent said to me, "Now, Alvin, there is one condition to this deal and that is that you never tell anyone where you got your gun. (When anyone asked where we got our gun, the answer, of course, was "Ferguson's Hardware in the Soo.") Joe added, "I have 42 other Methodist preachers and they will all want a gun." Thus we kept this secret locked to ourselves as long as Joe was in this world. This was quite a prize for a travelling preacher who loved the woods and game.

If anyone wants to go through this world without making enemies, there is a simple formula he must adopt: Say nothing; Do nothing; and Be nothing! *(Methodist Observer)*

TOO MANY NAMES

When father was young he rode a bicycle almost everywhere. He wore a jacket-type shirt that was seldom buttoned. As he rode in the wind the tail of the shirt would fly out behind him . . . The kids quite naturally noticed this and called him "Dickie, Dickie Doten, with his shirt-tail a-floatin'."

Later, as a growing boy in his early teens, his father and the community called him "Sonnie."

As an adult his first professional nickname was that of "Methodism's Sky Pilot." This name was affectionately given him when he was travelling over 15 counties in the Upper Peninsula of Michigan. He was a roving missionary, always on the move. When he could get back home to his family was a happy time. Mostly he was known as "The Portable Preacher."

Later, the Chippewa Indians adopted him into their tribe and gave him the name of Negonasah, meaning, The Leading Bird. (Mother always laughed at that Indian name. She said she had known for a long time that he was the "Leading Goose" in the family.)

In later years he became known as "The Trouble Man, or the Trouble Shooter." He was given special assignments in churches that were in some type of financial difficulty. I can't recall that he ever failed to help the people bring *their* church out of its financial slump and into the light of financial success and solvency once more. (In fact he helped organize and promote the building and rebuilding of several church buildings in his lifetime of service.)

Humorous stories went with him wherever he roamed. People's homes he always visited. Hospital rooms were just someplace that he regularly visited.

He always managed, somehow, to help congregations erect cathedrals while he was assisting the people in looking up at the steeple of the church, the House of God, his personal house and home on this planet.

—Marné Doten Dyer

After conference in late June, a church received a new minister. The following Monday, after the clergyman had preached his first sermon, he took it into the local newspaper. He said, "I would like to have this printed to help establish myself in this new community." (And, presumably to help draw *better crowds* the following Sunday.)

The newspaper, however, printed only the first half of the sermon. (This was before the linotype, when each letter had to be set individually.) Indignant, the preacher went to the newspaper office and asked, "Why on earth did you print only the first half of my sermon?"

The answer came back from the editor, "There was no way we could possibly have printed your entire sermon in this issue. Because, you see, we just ran out of the letter *I.*"

(Older Than I and Unknown)

A TRIBUTE TO THE AUTHOR
FROM A DAUGHTER

A good and gentle man retires today!
A world leader?
A military hero?
A statesman?
No.
But, in his own way,
A remarkable square.

A man who did square things
Like . . .
Paying his bills,
Ignoring credit, for cash,
Encouraging the young,
Marrying the "Dearly Beloved,"
Calling on the elderly,
Comforting the ill and bereaved,
Praying for all
As he
Cared for his family
And
God's family.

Interests, unlimited,
Were his.
Money, he liked.
He liked to earn it,
To save it,
To invest it.
But,
Most of all,
He liked to encourage
People to

Give it
To his church . . .
Your church.

Work, he thrived on!
Gardens, he planted.
Raspberries, he catered to.
Trees, he pruned.
Roses, he cultivated.
Nature, he worshipped.

Letters, he wrote.
Stamps, he collected.
Equipment, he repaired.
Photographs, he snapped.
Pictures, he etched.
Picnics and pot-lucks, he enjoyed.
Laughter, he cultivated.
Stories, he told.
Books, he carried with him.
Newspapers, he read.
The Bible, he lived by.

Music, he appreciated . . .
Particularly Gospel music.
"'Above the Hills of Time'
You can
Always hear music,
If you listen," he said.

Candles, he adored
Because
He created a light
In the spirit of man
With the flame of a candle.

People, he loved.
He surrounded himself with people.
"All around you," he said,
"Are people
Pressing their faces

Against the mirror of Time,
Seeking some little
'Furlinghetti-like
Initiation of Immortality'
Reach out,
And
Touch them."

Living with him was
Sometimes very emotional.
It was often wearisome
Trying to keep up with him.
(No one ever knew
where his energy came from!)
But, no matter what
We went through together
As a family,
In the end . . .
It was, somehow, inspirational.

He has known illnesses,
Struggle,
Hard work,
And
Defeat.
Yet, I have never heard him
Complain
About his lot.

He compensated for his small frame
By painting a picture called
PERSEVERANCE.
He kept this picture before him
On the wall of his world.
"Never be intimidated by anyone
Except your Heavenly Father," he
said.

He retires today
With silver memories
Woven into his "Golden Years."
Some of his beautiful days

Have been right here at Empire.
Here he has known some of
Christ's Chosen.
For your cooperation
Loyalty and love
His family will be ever grateful.

For Alice,
My sister, Doreen,
And brother, Donn,
We say "Thank you
For what you have given to him."

He retires today
But
He will never be unemployed.
His employer will be with him
Always.
For he is a "man of the Cloth."
He sees the "Crisis of Western Will"
As basically religious.
And, therefore,
He is just one of those men
Who will
"Tell Salvation's Story
Again and Again."
God . . .
Never EVACUATES
Nor
Can he,
Or WE.

—Marne Doten Dyer, Rochester, Indiana
(Donn's twin sister)
October 17, 1976